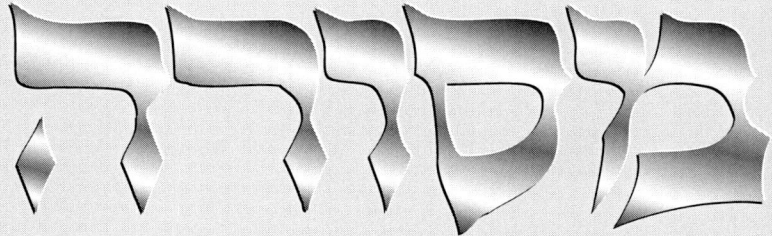

ArtScroll History Series®

Rabbi Nosson Scherman / Rabbi Meir Zlotowitz
General Editors

JOURNEY *to* JERUSALEM

THE HISTORIC VISIT
OF THE
MINCHAS ELUZAR
OF MUNKACS זצ"ל
TO THE
SABA KADISHA זצ"ל

Published by
Mesorah Publications, ltd.

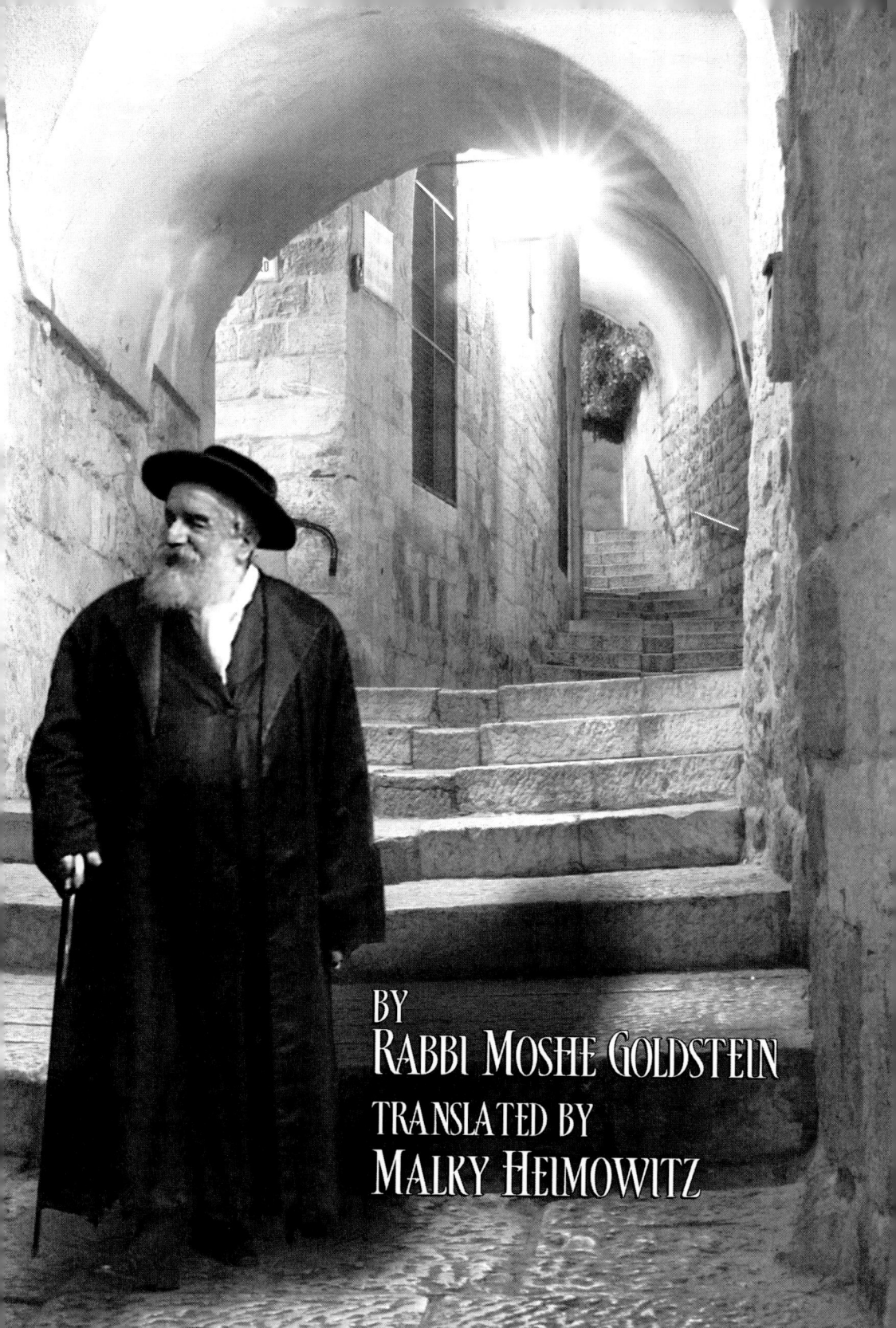

BY
RABBI MOSHE GOLDSTEIN

TRANSLATED BY
MALKY HEIMOWITZ

FIRST EDITION
First Impression … January 2009
Second Impression … May 2019

Published and Distributed by
MESORAH PUBLICATIONS, LTD.
4401 Second Avenue / Brooklyn, N.Y 11232

Distributed in Europe by
LEHMANNS
Unit E, Viking Business Park
Rolling Mill Road
Jarow, Tyne & Wear, NE32 3DP
England

Distributed in Australia and New Zealand by
GOLDS WORLDS OF JUDAICA
3-13 William Street
Balaclava, Melbourne 3183
Victoria, Australia

Distributed in Israel by
SIFRIATI / A. GITLER — BOOKS
POB 2351
Bnei Brak 51122

Distributed in South Africa by
KOLLEL BOOKSHOP
Northfield Centre, 17 Northfield Avenue
Glenhazel 2196, Johannesburg, South Africa

ARTSCROLL® HISTORY SERIES
JOURNEY TO JERUSALEM
© *Copyright 2009, by* MESORAH PUBLICATIONS, Ltd.
4401 Second Avenue / Brooklyn, N.Y. 11232 / (718) 921-9000 / www.artscroll.com

Typography by CompuScribe at ArtScroll Studios, Ltd.
Printed in the United States of America
Bound by Sefercraft, Quality Bookbinders, Ltd., Brooklyn N.Y. 11232

We dedicate this volume
to the memory of our beloved parents

Abraham Vegh
אברהם אלטר בן משה ע"ה
נפטר כ"ג אייר תשנ"א

Serena Vegh
שרה בת מרדכי ע"ה
נפטרה י'ג אייר תשס"ח

Shmuel Weiss
שמואל בן יעקב ע"ה
נפטר י"א ניסן תשנ"ז

Golda Weiss
גאלדה בת שמואל שמעלקע ע"ה
נפטרה כ"ד אלול תשנ"ד

Louis Yager
יהודה אריה בן אהרן הלוי ע"ה
נפטר כ"ט ניסן תשמ"ג

תנצב"ה

They came to America as survivors, and worked long and hard to create families in the image of the world that was lost. They let nothing stand in the way of the chinuch of their children. They succeeded.

We are resolved to keep their aspirations alive.

Moshe Mordechai (Mutty) and Shoshy Vegh,
Shmuli and Chanie, Yehuda Yehoshua and Tova,
Moshe Eluzar and Yaffa, and families

Eliyohu Issac (Robby) and Rozzy Vegh,
David and Miriam, Yaakov and Tolsie,
Shalom and Reena, and families, and Ariella

It was our honor to recently dedicate the new Hebrew edition of Mass'os Yerushalayim, and now to dedicate this, the first English translation of this classic, which contains many additions. We are especially proud to do so as a token of our enormous gratitude and respect for the Admor of Munkacs,

Hagaon Hatzaddik Harav Moshe Yehuda Leib Rabinovich שליט"א.

Our parents in Europe basked in the light of the tzaddikim of Krula, Apsha, Kashau, and Klemintov. Our closeness to the Admor of Munkacs — his wisdom, Torah, Avodah, tischen, middos, and personal relationships with ourselves, our children, and grandchildren — unite us with the sanctity of our pre-War origins. In times of joy and need, he is a source of inspiration and strength to us and thousands more around the world. May Hashem Yisbarach bless him with many years of good health and strength to continue his service to Klal Yisrael.

The Vegh Families
Staten Island and Lawrence, New York

Publisher's Preface

W̲e are honored to publish this classic account of the meeting of two spiritual giants of the pre-War generations. It was not only a meeting of two great men, it was a meeting of two worlds, the world of European Chassidus and the world of Sephardic Kabbalah.

In Czechoslovakia (present-day Ukraine), and throughout the world of Torah and Chassidus, the name Munkacs symbolized Torah greatness, fervent *avodas Hashem,* and uncompromising, unyielding loyalty to the *mesorah* of its holy forebears, since the *B'nai Yisas'char,* who are listed in this volume. The Gaon and Tzaddik, Harav Chaim Eluzar Shapira, led his chassidim with wisdom, compassion, and firmness. His many volumes of *Minchas Eluzar* were recognized everywhere as brilliant and authoritative works of halachah.

In Jerusalem, the Saba Kadisha was one of the wonders of the age. The Gaon and Tzaddik, Harav Shlomo Eliezer Elfandri, was well over 100 years of age — according to some, he was 120! — and after earning the reverence of communities in Turkey and Iraq as a profound Torah scholar and Kabbalist, he settled in the Holy City. Despite his advanced age, his mind was clear and, like the Minchas Eluzar he was a Torah giant who fearlessly spoke out against those who tried to bend the *mesorah* to make it compatible with current political "realities."

The more the Minchas Eluzar became aware of the towering stature of the Saba Kadisha, the more he longed to travel to Jerusalem to meet him. It was said that the Munkacser Rav even practiced speaking the Sephardic pronunciation of *lashon hakodesh* so that he would be able to converse easily with Harav Elfandri when they met.

Letters went from Munkacs to Jerusalem requesting permission to visit. For a long time, the Saba Kadisha answered that the time was not ripe. Then, finally, the elderly sage acceded to the Rebbe's request, and invited him to "come in joy." Enthusiastically, the Munkacser Rav began preparations for the trip, which took place after Pesach, 1930. Their many meetings were characterized by mutual respect and affection, so much so that many distinguished people in Eretz Yisrael were astounded at how the perceived "barriers" between Sephardim and Ashkenazim vanished.

A distinguished disciple of the Rebbe was Rabbi Moshe Goldstein, who accompanied him on the trip to Jerusalem and kept an extensive diary of the trip and its aftermath. Entitled *Mass'os Yerusalayim*, it was first published in 1931 and most recently in 2004. It is noteworthy to mention that most of the photographs in this book are from the original collection taken by Reb Yehoshua Yehuda Lowinger, one of the participants on the Rebbe's journey to Jerusalem.

In response to requests from English-speaking people, this translation was prepared and augmented with biographies of the Minchas Eluzar and the Saba Kadisha. We are confident that the public will applaud this rare opportunity to become acquainted with two giants of our past. Their warm relationship with one another and their passionate endeavors to prepare the way for the coming of *Mashiach* and the final Redemption will inspire readers. Let us hope that their example will enhance mutual respect among our people and spur the repentance that will deliver us from the throes of spiritual and physical exile.

ACKNOWLEDGMENTS

This work has been sponsored and dedicated by **Mr. and Mrs. Moshe Mordechai (Mutty) Vegh** and **Mr. and Mrs. Eliyohu Issac (Robby) Vegh.** They have become very devoted to the present Munkacser Rav shlita, and with his blessing have undertaken to make this volume available to the broad, English-speaking public. The Veghs are long-time good friends of ArtScroll/Mesorah. They have dedicated previous ArtScroll volumes and we are proud to continue the association with this volume, *Journey to Jerusalem.*

We are grateful to **Rabbi Fishel Rabinovich,** who has been a guiding light of the work and has provided his full cooperation and constructive suggestions throughout.

The beautiful translation was done by **Mrs. Malky Heimowitz** of Jerusalem. As an interesting by-product of her fine work, she learned that her great-grandparents, Shmuel and Chaya Klein, were Munkacser chassidim who moved from Hungary to Jerusalem in the 1920's. During the Rebbe's stay in Jerusalem, Reb Shmuel was his *baal tefillah* and Mrs. Klein was his cook.

The Vegh families express their thanks to **Rabbi Yaakov Marcus,** Rabbi Emeritus of the Young Israel of Staten Island and founder of Raishit Yerushalayim in Beit Shemesh. Rabbi Marcus introduced the

Veghs to ArtScroll many years ago, which led to their dedication of *Rosh Hashanah*, in the Holiday series, and the Tishah B'Av *Kinnos*.

The Vegh family would like to thank and acknowledge their rav in Staten Island, **Rabbi Yaakov Lehrfield**, for his help, friendship, and guidance at all times.

Reb Meir Yosef Frankel made available his wealth of photographs from the period, many of which have never before been published. His son, **Reb Usher**, gave much time to fitting the photos into the appropriate parts of the narrative and providing captions. Their generosity and efforts contributed immeasurably to the beauty and value of this volume.

Our esteemed colleague Eli Kroen designed the cover with his customary taste and skill.

Mrs. Tzini Fruchthandler designed the book and Mrs. Mindy Stern proofread and made valuable suggestions. We are grateful to them both.

Our colleague Shmuel Blitz, director of our Jerusalem office, is an integral part of our work and accomplishments, and a skilled liaison between Jerusalem and New York.

We express our appreciation to Mendy Herzberg, who supervised the production. He shuns the limelight, but the final product is testimony to his competence.

Finally, we thank Hashem Yisbarach for giving us the honor of presenting this precious slice of history to His people.

Rabbi Meir Zlotowitz   Rabbi Nosson Scherman
Teves 5769 / January 2009

TABLE OF CONTENTS

THE LIFE OF A GIANT: THE "MINCHAS ELUZAR"

The holy Rebbe, the Minchas Eluzar

The Minchas Eluzar

The Minchas Eluzar, R' Chaim Eluzar Shapira, was the scion of a generations-long chain of great Jewish leaders. He was the son of R' Tzvi Hirsch Shapira, the author of *Darkei Teshuvah*; the son of R' Shlomo Shapira, the author of *Shem Shlomo*; the son of R' Eluzar Shapira, the author of *Yod'ei Binah*; the son of R' Tzvi Elimelech Shapira, the author of *Bnei Yissas'char*.

The Bnei Yissas'char was the forebear of a distinguished, multi-branched lineage. He studied under two holy tzaddikim, R' Menachem Mendele of Rimanov and R' Yaakov Yitzchak, the Chozeh of Lublin, both of whom were disciples of R' Elimelech of Lizhensk, the author of *Noam Elimelech*. R' Elimelech was a disciple of R' Ber, the Maggid of Mezritch, who was a disciple and the successor of the Baal Shem Tov.

Matzeivah of the holy Bnei Yissas'char in Dynow, Poland

The Minchas Eluzar was also a descendant of the authors of *Pnei Yehoshua* and *Meginei Shlomo*, through his great-grandmother, Rebbetzin Toba Chava — the daughter of R' Yehoshua Heshel, and the wife of the *Yod'ei Binah*.

His grandmother, Rebbetzin Chaya Frima Rivka, the wife of the *Shem Shlomo*, was the daughter of R' Yekusiel Shmelke of Sassov, who was the son of R' Moshe Yehudah Leib of Sassov and the son-in-law of R' Reuven Yaffe. R' Reuven Yaffe was a great-grandson of the author of *Levush*, and R' Isaac Charif, a contemporary of the Baal Shem Tov and the author of *Tiferes Yisrael*.

His mother, Rebbetzin Esther, was the daughter of R' Chanina Horowitz, head of the rabbinical court (*Av Beis Din*) of Olinov. R' Chanina was the son of R' Yaakov, *Av Beis Din* of Melitz and the son-in-law of his uncle, R' Eliezer of Dzhikov. R' Yaakov and R' Eliezer were sons of the great R' Naftali of Ropshitz, who was the son of R' Menachem Mendel, *Av Beis Din* of Linsk, who was the son-in-law of R' Yitzchak, *Av Beis Din* of Hamburg. The family traced its lineage all the way back to Shefatya ben Avital, who was descended from King David.

"You Will Have Children"

The Rebbe's parents were childless for over six years. On the last day of Pesach 5631/1871, when his father, the Darkei Teshuvah, was in the company of the holy Divrei Chaim of Sanz, he asked for a blessing for children, and the Divrei Chaim blessed him, saying, "You will have children." And so it was.

The Minchas Eluzar was an only child, and for many years, he, too, had no children. However, he always believed in the Divrei Chaim's blessing that his father would have children — "children" in the plural — and since his father had had only one child, the Minchas Eluzar interpreted the blessing to include grandchildren as well. And indeed, his interpretation was correct: the blessing came true.

Already in his youth, the Rebbe displayed outstanding abilities. When he was 2, his grandmother began teaching him the letters of the *aleph-beis,* and he learned all the letters in one day. The next day, she began teaching him *"komatz aleph uh,"* and he continued on his own: from *"komatz beis buh"* until *"komatz tav tuh."*

When he was 8, he became engaged to the daughter of R' Shraga Yair of Bialebzig. At the *tenaim* celebration, he delivered a *pilpul* (Talmudic

The holy Sanzer Rav, Rav Chaim Halberstam, author of Divrei Chaim

discourse) that demonstrated to his future father-in-law his proficiency in Talmud.

A notebook of Torah novellae that he began to write at the age of 10 was found in his library. Before his bar mitzvah, he began to write a work on the laws of tefillin, which became the basis for his *sefer, Os Chaim.* Immediately after his bar mitzvah he began putting on Rabbeinu Tam tefillin, as his grandfather the Bnei Yissas'char had instructed his descendants.

When he was 15, he celebrated his wedding in Tchebin, Poland. After the chuppah, his grandfather, the Shem Shlomo, proclaimed that the heavenly angels who had come to participate in the celebration were astounded to see that there are still such exalted individuals in the lower world, as this chassan.

For several years after his marriage, the young Minchas Eluzar immersed himself in Torah and service of G-d in his father-in-law's home in Bialebzig. During that period, he visited many of the tzaddikim and Torah leaders in Russia and Poland, and his reputation as a budding Torah giant began to spread. When he was 25, R' Yechezkel of Shiniva said of him that his growth in Torah each day was so great that if a person had heard *divrei Torah* from him one day, they would not recognize him the next, since his greatness in Torah grew to unimaginable heights every day.

In 5653/1893, the Shem Shlomo passed away, and the Darkei Teshuvah assumed the rabbinic leadership of Munkacs. This opened a new chapter in the Rebbe's life. He began helping his father oversee religious affairs in Munkacs and the surrounding areas. Several times, his father assigned important matters to him, confident that he would attend to them in the best way possible.

In 5664/1904, the Rebbe was officially appointed *Av Beis Din* of Munkacs. He never took payment for adjudicating *dinei Torah*, nor did he accept money from the chassidim who came to his father.

In 5666/1906, twenty years after his marriage, he had not yet been blessed with children. He divorced his righteous wife so that he could remarry and have children. About a year later, he married the daughter of R' Yaakov Moshe of Komarna. In 5675/1915, she gave birth to the Rebbe's only child, Chaya Frima Rivka.

The holy Rebbe, Rav Tzvi Hirsch Shapira, author of Darkei Teshuvah

HIS WORKS

In 5662/1902, when he was but 30 years old, he published the first volume of his *Responsa Minchas Eluzar*. Great Torah leaders gave the *sefer* their endorsement. This *sefer* earned him a reputation as a Torah genius — for his breadth of knowledge, his analytical ability, his formidable memory, and his decisive halachic rulings. This *sefer* propelled him into a leadership role and turned him into one of the foremost Torah leaders of the region.

That same year, he published the second volume of *Minchas Eluzar*, which further established his position as a noted *posek* to whom many leaders of the generation referred complex halachic questions. In later years, he published his other works: additional volumes of *Minchas Eluzar, Os Chaim V'Shalom, Nimukei Orach Chaim, Divrei Torah, Olas Tamid, Shaar Yissachar*, and other *sefarim*. His many works were accepted with respect and honor and they still occupy a distinguished place in the literature of Torah, halachah, and chassidus.

One of the few descriptions that he allowed to be inscribed on his tombstone was, "He authored many fine, valuable works." (In his will, the Rebbe forbade any praises or descriptions to be inscribed on his tombstone, except for those that he himself prescribed.)

RAV OF MUNKACS

After the Darkei Teshuvah passed away on the second day of Succos 5674/1914, there were those in Munkacs who wished to make the Minchas Eluzar's appointment as rav contingent upon his agreement that secular studies would be included in the curriculum. The Minchas Eluzar opposed these changes vehemently and declared publicly that he was prepared to give his life rather than change even one iota of the traditional educational system. At the end, truth prevailed, and he was elected rav of Munkacs by a majority of the city's residents.

The Minchas Eluzar served as the rav and *Av Beis Din* of Munkacs and its environs for almost twenty-five years. He oversaw all aspects of Jewish observance — kashrus, mikvaos, modesty of dress, marriages, boys' and girls' education, Shabbos, and more. He invested much effort into the construction of a beautiful Talmud Torah, which produced thousands of G-d-fearing students.

It soon became evident to the Jews of Munkacs that their rav was not only a giant in Torah but was also a saintly person and a miracle worker.

In 5674/1914, World War I broke out, and the fighting spread quickly from city to city. Before Rosh Hashanah 5675, sounds of war were heard near Munkacs, and the frightened residents were unsure whether to flee the city or remain. On the second day of Rosh Hashanah, when the Rebbe awoke, the verse, "There they will be stricken with terror, a terror that never was" (*Tehillim* 53:6) came to his lips. He interpreted this according to the teaching of the Sages in *Berachos* that when a verse comes to a person's mind upon awakening, it is a degree of prophecy. He therefore announced that there is no reason to fear and that the residents should remain in the city. And that is what happened. Many of the villages surrounding Munkacs were captured by the Russians, but, miraculously, they retreated before reaching Munkacs. As a result of this incident, the Rebbe became known as a holy tzaddik, and even the gentiles admired and respected him greatly.

About three months later, the Russian army returned and advanced upon Munkacs once again. This time, the commander of the local force went to the Minchas Eluzar to hear with his own ears the promise that the enemy would not invade. When the Rebbe reiterated his promise, the commander was incredulous, and he asked if the Rebbe had secret ties with the enemy. "These matters are known to me clearly," the Rebbe replied. Then he added, "Just as I do not intervene in military matters, you should not intervene in matters of the heart." At the end, the Russians retreated a second time, and the Rebbe became even more revered throughout the region.

During the war years, refugees streamed into Munkacs, many of them seeking the Rebbe's blessing and advice. They would give the *pidyon* (monetary offering) customarily given to chassidic rebbes, but not only did he refuse to accept this money, he also went

A rebbe teaching aleph-beis in the cheder in Munkacs

Aerial view of the city of Munkacs

personally to the homes of wealthy people to collect money for the refugees. He even risked his life to rescue those refugees who did not have identity papers and were therefore suspect in the eyes of the authorities.

The Rebbe's efforts to help his fellow Jews during and after the war years were not limited to providing physical assistance. On Rosh Hashanah 5679/1918, before the blowing of the shofar, the Minchas Eluzar cried out loudly, "All of the ministering angels of the nations who are sitting above should fall down below! How can these evil ones sit above and judge us?"

Then he explained what he meant. "If the Jewish people would emerge meritorious in judgment and the Redemption would come this year, the nations would be judged and they would all fall. So they have a vested interest in speaking ill of the Jewish people, and their testimony against us is not valid."

It was clear to everyone present that the Rebbe was waging a battle in the upper worlds against the ministering angels of the nations. Indeed, during that year several kings and high-ranking ministers were deposed.

The Rebbe also fought valiantly against those who wished to undermine the foundations of Judaism, namely, the various factions of the *Haskalah* (Enlightenment) and the Zionist movement. He once said of himself that he is a spark of the soul of R' Eluzar the son of R' Shimon bar Yochai, who "came to rid the vineyard of the thorns." He also tried to convince Jewish leaders in Poland not to found the Agudas Yisrael movement. He established a special committee in Hungary that forbade joining any of the parties that had ties to Zionism.

In 5682/1922, he founded Yeshivah Darkei Teshuvah in Munkacs, named for his father. The goal of the yeshivah was to teach pure Torah, unadulterated by any secular ideologies. Fortunate were those who saw the Rebbe, appearing like an angel of God, entering the beis medrash to give *shiurim* and to test the talmidim. He imbued the talmidim with love of Torah and fear of God. The yeshivah developed and flourished, producing many rabbanim and *poskim*.

The Rebbe displayed intense, genuine love for his students, treating them like a father. Following the example of R' Akiva Eiger, he did not refer to them as "talmidim" — for "who knows who learned more from whom?"

Bachurim of the Munkacser Yeshivah, pre WW II

Bringing Mashiach

The Minchas Eluzar yearned intensely for the arrival of Mashiach. Already when he was a child of 10 he wrote in the introduction to his notebook of Torah novellae, "May we all merit the arrival of the Mashiach, may he come speedily in our days." Many of his fiery, stirring discourses focused on the need to repent in order to merit the Redemption, and these discourses penetrated deeply into the hearts of his listeners.

The Rebbe wished to impress upon people that whenever a person does a good deed, and whenever he refrains from doing something wrong, he brings the footsteps of Mashiach closer — and this is the goal of the entire universe. He would often quote the words of Ridvaz, that tzaddikim who exerted themselves to bring about the Redemption would be among the first to rise during the Resurrection of the Dead. In his inspiring discourses during the Days of Awe and on Shavuos, he would frequently call upon the people to be prepared to make any sacrifice in order to bring the Redemption.

Once, on Hoshana Rabbah, before the recitation of the phrase, *"Hoshana lemaan zichrach —* Save now, for the sake of Your remembrance," he related the story told about several tzaddikim who promised dur-

The holy Rebbe, the Minchas Eluzar, on Hoshana Rabbah

ing their lifetimes that when they would go up to the next world they would refuse to enter Gan Eden. Instead, they would storm the heavens until the Redemption would arrive. When they came to the next world, however, they were distracted in various ways, until they forgot their promise and entered Gan Eden. "That is why," the Minchas Eluzar continued, "we pray *Hoshana lemaan zichrach* — Hashem, *You* should remember us! Do not forget our suffering in Exile. We cry out to You to save us!"

The Rebbe used every opportunity to speak positively of the Jewish people and ask Hashem to redeem His children speedily. Once, when he traveled to Germany for medical reasons, the time came to recite *Kiddush Levanah*, but the sky was cloudy. The Rebbe stood and waited until well after midnight, in the hope of seeing the moon. Suddenly, he saw a clean-shaven Jew in a window in one of the nearby houses calling joyously to his friends, "The moon is here!" The Rebbe was thrilled to see the love of the mitzvah displayed by the German Jews, who waited up for *Kiddush Levanah*. He used this incident as grounds for advocating on behalf of the Jewish people and begging Hashem to redeem them from exile.

He was deeply pained by the suffering of the exile, and he would cry and lament over the plight of his people. In his work, *Divrei Torah*, he explains the Talmud's description of the suffering that Mashiach will endure in a way that reflects how intensely he felt the pain of exile. The Talmud (*Sanhedrin* 98b) says that if Mashiach were alive today, he would be like Rabbeinu HaKadosh (who suffered ailments — *Rashi*). If he is among the dead, the Talmud continues, he is like Daniel (upon whom it was decreed to suffer in the lions' den — *Rashi*). The Minchas Eluzar points out that Daniel was in the lions' den for only one night, and during that time he experienced a miracle: the lions accorded him honor. So what suffering did Daniel endure?

Daniel, the Minchas Eluzar explains, was privy to the time that Mashiach would arrive, but he was told (*Daniel* 12:13), "As for you, go to [your] end; you will rest — then arise for your portion at the End of Days."

"Daniel was shown in a prophetic vision how very long it would be until the Redemption, and then he was told to rest — in the grave

— for he would not see the Redemption in his days. He would arise only at then End of Days, during the Resurrection, together with the other tzaddikim. There can be no greater suffering than that!"

Chassidim in the court of the Minchas Eluzar

UNTIL THE ARRIVAL OF THE REDEEMER

During World War I, the Rebbe considered the hostilities between the various empires to be an indicator of the war of Gog and Magog, which will precede the Redemption. He urged his generation to repent in preparation for the arrival of Mashiach, and not to pray only for the war to end. "The thrust of our prayers has to be that the Redemption of the Jewish people should arrive," he would constantly emphasize.

Other rabbanim wanted to declare a public fast to pray for the war to end and for peace to return to the nations, but the Rebbe was opposed, arguing that the focus of the prayers has to be for rectification of sins and for Redemption from exile. He compared the proposal of the rabbis to a woman in labor who, instead of praying that the baby should be born healthy, prays only that the labor pains should stop.

One morning, the Rebbe awoke with bite marks on his hands. He explained that during the night he had had a frightening dream. Satan had come to him in the form of a large dog, and demanded that he stop pleading for the Redemption to come speedily. Satan threatened to harm him if he did not comply, but the Rebbe did not give in to the threats. He resisted with all his might, until Satan finally bit his hand. When the Rebbe related this to his family, he declared that he would never yield to Satan and that he would continue in this manner until the Redemption came.

In 5693/1933, when the Nazis rose to power in Germany, the Minchas Eluzar was asked if it would be proper to call a public fast. He replied, "Satan is trying to blind us to the truth that these are the birth pangs of Mashiach. When we repent, we will merit to be redeemed." He added that he had a tradition from his holy ancestors that the purpose of the war would be solely to spur the Jewish people to repent and thereby hasten the Redemption.

ABOUT WHAT WAS HE MOST SCRUPULOUS?

The Talmud (*Shabbos* 118b) states that a person asked his friend, "About which matter was your father the most scrupulous?" *Noam Elimelech* (*Parashas Beshalach*) explains that it is impossible for a person to be equally scrupulous in the fulfillment of every aspect and detail of every mitzvah. If, however, a person is scrupulous in the fulfillment of all aspects and details of even a single mitzvah, this mitzvah will earn him the Divine assistance that will enable him to perform all the mitzvos. (See *Zekan Beisi* of the Rebbe of Komarna to *Avos* 2:10.)

When discussing this idea, the Rebbe added that when the Day of Judgment arrives, the one mitzvah that he performed scrupulously will be his advocate and protect him. This is the meaning of the verse (*Iyov* 33:23-24), "If someone will have but a single defending angel out of a thousand to declare his uprightness on his behalf, then [G-d] will be gracious and say, 'Redeem him from going down to the grave.'" It is enough, the Rebbe said, to have the advocate created by scrupulous observance of even a single mitzvah to speak well of a person, and in this way he will be "redeemed from descending to the grave."

"I thought to myself," the Rebbe continued, "that if I have merited to perform one negative commandment scrupulously, it would be the mitzvah, 'You shall not tremble before any man' (*Devarim* 1:17). Among the positive mitzvos, the one I would say that I fulfilled, with Hashem's help, would be the mitzvah of 'I anticipate every day that Mashiach will come.' Even though he may delay, I will wait for him every day, every hour and every moment." Indeed, if someone would but mention Mashiach, tears of pain would stream from the Rebbe's eyes.

As the greatest Torah authority of the region, the Rebbe carried many public responsibilities on his shoulders, in matters of religion and Torah in particular. He would occasionally invite the leading rabbanim of the area to solicit their opinions and to instruct them regarding relevant matters.

Once, a conference was scheduled to take place in the capital city of Budapest, and many of the rabbanim of the region were invited to participate. Prior to the conclave, the Rebbe called an urgent meeting of leading rabbanim who were close to him to prepare for the conference, for he feared that the participants would call for changes in certain traditions. It became apparent during the meeting that the rabbanim did not see the potential dangers of a certain matter, and he spoke passionately about its importance.

The tzaddik of Shopron, who was present, related that even though it was a private meeting, a pauper managed to enter without the *gabbaim* noticing. He extended his hand to the Rebbe for a contribution, and the Rebbe put his hand into his pocket while continuing to speak. Without pausing, he took out a bill and gave it

The holy Minchas Eluzar (third from right) with rabbanim in Marienbad, Czechoslovakia

to the pauper — for when he gave tzedakah he never looked at the denomination of the bill he was giving. Apparently, the bill was a big one, for the pauper was delighted when he saw it. He exclaimed, "The Rebbe should live to see Mashiach speedily!"

Although he was in the midst of speaking heatedly, when he heard Mashiach being mentioned and himself being blessed to see his coming, the Rebbe abruptly stopped speaking. It was as if a new spirit entered him. Teardrops began to stream from his eyes, and he said, "*Gevald*! When, when will we live to see Mashiach? Hashem should help that we should see him soon, as soon as possible, together with all of Klal Yisrael!"

He was so emotional that he could not pick up where he had stopped, and he gave the floor to another rabbi until he regained his self-control and was able to continue speaking.

"JEWISH PAIN"

Towards the end of the Rebbe's life, he was hospitalized in Budapest, far from home, and asked the doctor for permission to daven with a *minyan* on Shabbos. At the time, anti-Semitism was intensifying steadily, and the hospital administration turned down his request. His doctor knew him personally, however, and out of reverence for him said that he was prepared to assume the responsibility of permitting the *minyan*, but on the condition that there be only ten people and that they would abide by the hospital's requirement that the other patients' rest not be disturbed. The Rebbe was very happy, and he blessed the doctor with a long life.

For the Friday night prayers, a *minyan* of prominent men who had promised to abide by hospital protocol arrived. They began Minchah with Psalm 107: "Those redeemed by Hashem will say, those whom He redeemed from the hand of distress, and whom He gathered from the lands, from east and from west, from north and from the sea...Then they cried out to Hashem in their distress." As the Rebbe said these words, he tried not to raise his voice, but before long tears poured from his eyes and a cry escaped his lips. Afraid that he would be sanctioned for permitting the *minyan*, the doctor rushed to the room and asked the Rebbe to keep his promise not to raise his voice.

After Shabbos, the doctor asked the Rebbe about his behavior during the Shabbos prayers. "Even if you had not given your promise," the doctor told him, "you should have been considerate enough not to disturb the rest of other patients."

The Rebbe replied, "When we discussed this matter, I understood that the hospital's insistence on total silence was an absolute rule, and therefore I promised not to violate it. But then, at night, I realized that this is not the case. I had just fallen asleep when I heard terrible screams. I could not sleep most of the night because of those screams."

The doctor smiled and said, "The Rebbe is a wise man — how can he say such a thing? The person who screamed had been run over by a car and his legs were crushed. He was brought to the hospital in a terrible state, and he was screaming in pain. In general, however, there is absolute silence in the hospital, to allow the patients to rest undisturbed."

To this, the Rebbe answered, "Honorable doctor, you studied in prestigious schools, and you were taught about various types of pain and illnesses — headaches, stomachaches, broken limbs, etc. But did they ever teach you about 'Jewish pain'? Do you have any idea how great is the pain of a Jew who is waiting thousands of years for the arrival of the Mashiach and the Redemption? Every year, the Jew says, 'This is the year that we will be redeemed,' but we still have not been redeemed. You will never feel the heartache of a Jewish soul who seeks the peace of Jerusalem and waits anxiously for the time when 'Those redeemed by Hashem will say, those whom He redeemed from the hand of distress, and whom He gathered from the lands.' This is a deep-seated pain that bursts forth unrestrained, and no promises in the world can silence those screams of pain."

Perek HaBayis VeHa'aliyah

When one of the Rebbe's most prominent students was a *bachur*, he returned to his hometown after a *zeman* in the yeshivah. Asked which *perek* he had just studied, he replied, "I studied *Perek HaBayis VeHa'aliyah* (lit., The House and the Attic) — for I saw with my own eyes a true tzaddik who lives down below in this dark exile, in a house, but whose thoughts are always above, clinging to his Creator and working to rectify the world and bring about the Redemption."

The Rebbe's students and chassidim saw clearly how true this was. But despite his great desire and prodigious efforts to bring about the Redemption, he never abandoned his "house" — his flock of chassidim. He displayed fatherly love and concern for each of them, rejoicing in their joys and helping them during times of distress. His love for his fellow Jew was boundless.

Once, a chassid of his was slandered before the government. Facing a difficult trial and the possibility of a severe punishment,

he decided to travel to the Rebbe to receive his blessing. It was before Purim, and several of his friends were planning to travel to a different Rebbe. They convinced him to join them, since he did not usually spend Purim with the Minchas Eluzar.

Before Shavuos, this chassid traveled to the Minchas Eluzar for Yom Tov, as he usually did. When he arrived, he saw that the Rebbe was upset with him. (Chassidic rebbes were insistent that chassidim not go to two rebbes. There is a tradition from the Bnei Yissas'char that the bond between a chassid and his Rebbe is a sacred thing that may not be tampered with. Just as a person cannot have two fathers, a chassid cannot have two rebbes, for a rebbe is like a father.)

When the chassid came into the Rebbe on Motza'ei Yom Tov and told him about his trial, he apologized and explained, "The Rebbe is concerned only about the Redemption. Every time I visit the Rebbe, he is preoccupied with the holy *Shechinah*, with Mashiach, and with the Redemption, so I felt I could not speak to the Rebbe about my trial. I decided that I would have two rebbes," the chassid concluded, "one for Mashiach and one for my own troubles."

The Rebbe smiled. "It is true that I am always concerned that we should merit the final Redemption. But that is not at the expense of a Jew's pain or distress. Am I better than the holy *Shechinah*? Although the *Shechinah* is in exile, when a Jew suffers, the *Shechinah* feels the pain and says, 'I am in distress because of my head, I am in distress because of my arm.' So too, even though the pain of Mashiach is more painful than anything else, I still feel the pain of every individual. I do not forget anyone."

LOVE OF ZION

The Rebbe's heart burned with an intense love of Eretz Yisrael. He yearned to travel to the Holy Land, especially after he developed a special bond through correspondence with the Saba Kadisha, R' Shlomo Eliezer Elfandri of Jerusalem. He spent thirteen days in Eretz Yisrael, which, he explained, corresponded to the thirteen years that R' Shimon bar Yochai and his son R' Eluzar spent in the cave. During his visit, he met with the Saba Kadisha a number of times. On the fourth day of his stay, he arrived at the home of the Saba Kadisha and he asked that no one else should enter the house, for he wished to speak with the Saba Kadisha privately. From outside, however, the chassidim overheard the two tzaddikim discussing the Redemption.

The Rebbe asked, "When will Mashiach arrive?"

The Saba Kadisha turned around and motioned to the wall, and answered, "Behold, he is standing behind our wall!"

"Why is he standing behind our wall, rather than coming inside?" the Rebbe asked.

"Because the evil people of the generation are standing in the doorway and not allowing him in," the Saba Kadisha replied.

In a voice choked with tears the Rebbe asked, "Am I one of those who are delaying him?" His greatness and humility were evident at the same time.

The Rebbe returned home from Eretz Yisrael several days before Shavuos, soon after the passing of the Saba Kadisha. That Shavuos, a larger-than-usual crowd gathered to be in his presence, eager to hear what he would say about his trip to the Holy Land. During his regular *derashah* before *Akdamos*, the Rebbe said: "When I was in the Holy City of Jerusalem in the presence of the Saba Kadisha, I asked him when the Redeemer would arrive, and he replied, 'He is standing behind our wall!' There are several ways to interpret these words, but the main thing is that if we do *teshuvah* and return to Hashem with all our hearts, accepting the Torah joyously and following its dictates with love, then our salvation will arrive speedily.

"In the Mussaf of Yom Kippur," he continued, "we say, 'He has turned Mashiach away from us.' But Mashiach has never been sent to redeem us, so how can we say that he has been turned away from us? This year, the words 'He has turned Mashiach away from us' have been fulfilled, for Hashem has taken His anointed away."

The following Hoshana Rabbah, the Rebbe related that one Friday, the Baal Shem Tov called his student R' Leib, the Maggid of Polnoah, to accompany him on a journey. The two traveled by wagon for quite a distance, through forests and fields, and the journey was miraculously shortened for them, as often happened to the holy Baal Shem Tov. Finally, they came to a place where there was one house, and the Baal Shem Tov asked that the wagon be stopped. A man with a beautiful countenance came out of the house, and he and the Baal Shem Tov greeted one another joyously. The man urged the Baal Shem Tov to stay with him for Shabbos, but the Baal Shem Tov refused and returned home.

R' Leib wondered what was going on, but he did not ask any questions. Finally, the Baal Shem Tov turned to him and said, "Do you know who that man was? That was the Mashiach of our generation!"

R' Leib was astounded, and he asked the Baal Shem Tov, "If so, why didn't the Rebbe agree to stay with him for Shabbos?"

The Baal Shem Tov replied, "Because I saw that the sins of the generation have caused a decree that he will pass away this Shabbos, and I cannot bear to see Mashiach being taken from us."

After telling this story, the Rebbe concluded tearfully, "My dear brothers, you understand to whom my words allude — woe unto us! But even though, in our sins, Mashiach has been taken from us, we have faith in Hashem who lives eternally and is called 'my living Redeemer.' He is the true Redeemer, and He can redeem us speedily."

The Rebbe's sole intention in traveling to Eretz Yisrael was to hasten the Redemption, similar to the famous meeting between the Baal Shem Tov and the Ohr HaChaim HaKadosh. But the generation was not worthy, so the opportunity was lost.

"The Satan Has Prevailed"

In the last year of the Rebbe's life, when his health was deteriorating steadily, he conducted himself in mysterious ways. On the first day of Rosh Hashanah, he departed from his usual custom, refusing to daven with the congregation or conduct the *tisch*. While praying alone, he cried and pleaded with Hashem far more than he had done in previous years.

On the second day of Rosh Hashanah he said, "Next year, the Kohen Gadol will already daven in the Beis HaMikdash, and he can do better than I can." Throughout the following months, he hinted in various ways that he foresaw that something momentous would happen that year. But he did not explain what he meant.

בעז"הי.

התעוררו

לבקש רחמים מרובים

בבתי כנסיות ובבתי מדרשות
ובכל מקומות הקדושים

בעד גאון וצדיק הדור מאור הגולה
כ"ק עט"ר אדמו"ר ונשיא א' בתוכינו

רבינו חיים אלעזר בן אסתר
שליט"א

הגאב"ד ור"מ דעוב"י מונקאטש יצ"ו

לרפואה שלימה במהרה
בתושח"י אמן

הנהלת
כולל מונקאטש

דפוס קלוזר – ירושלים

Placard urging Yidden to gather and pray to beseech a refuah sheleimah for the holy Minchas Eluzar

On his father's yahrtzeit, at the grave, he said something unusual. After speaking about his battles against the heretics, he said, "We are fighting against them with all our might, literally sacrificing ourselves. But until when? There comes a time when we become tired!"

On Simchas Torah of that year, he related the well-known story of the tzaddikim of Kozhnitz, Rimanov, and Lublin, who endeavored in the year 5575/1815 to bring about the Redemption. Unfortunately, due to the sins of our people they did not succeed, and all of them passed away during that year.

Shortly before the Rebbe's passing, on the last Pesach of his life, his health was very precarious and he did not have the strength to perform his holy service the entire holiday. Several days after Pesach, however, he appeared to take a turn for the better. At that time, R' Shalom Eliezer of Ratzfert, the youngest son of the Sanzer Rav, came to visit him. When he entered the Rebbe's room, the Rebbe asked him to sit on his bed, and he held his hand during the entire visit. R' Shalom Eliezer said that he was returning from a trip to Sanz, where he had prayed at the grave of his father on his yahrtzeit — 25 Nissan. The Rebbe stopped him and said, "Members of my family can tell you that I knew it was the Rebbe's yahrtzeit, for I had a sign. On that day, I began to feel a bit better."

The Rebbe of Ratzfert,
Rav Shalom Eliezer Halberstam

R' Shalom Eliezer replied, "It is not surprising, for at the gravesite in Sanz were posted signs to pray for the recovery of Chaim Eluzar ben Esther. There were tens of thousands of Jews there, not one of whom did not pray for the Rebbe."

The Rebbe sighed, and said with bitter tears, "On such a great day and at such a holy place, all they had to pray for was the pain of a human being like me? They should have prayed for the pain of the holy *Shechinah* and begged for the Redemption — then we would have already been redeemed!"

The levayah of the holy Minchas Eluzar, 2 Sivan 5697

During those days, while he was suffering terribly, the Rebbe said, "The Satan has prevailed over me!" He did not live to see the Redemption, for he was taken to the heavens on 2 Sivan 5697/1937.

May his merit protect us and all of the Jewish people.

The Munkacser Rebbe Shlita at the kever of the Minchas Eluzar in Mukachevo, Ukraine, 2006

REBIRTH IN THE NEW WORLD

In the aftermath of Churban Europe, most people were sure the chassidic and Torah life of pre-War Europe was forever extinct. There would surely be isolated communities that would be relics of the past, but the thriving, vibrant, spiritually elevated life of the past would never be reborn — certainly not in the materialistic United States, where such life had never taken root, even before the War.

They were wrong. History would repeat itself. During the days of the First Beis HaMikdash, power-hungry Queen Asaliah tried to murder all the descendants of David HaMelech — even her own children and grandchildren. If she had succeeded, the royal line from David to Mashiach would have been severed, but the Hashgachah intervened. Unbeknownst to her, the infant prince, Yoash, was rescued and kept hidden in the Beis HaMikdash complex for several years, until he was old enough to be proclaimed the new king. Hashem protects Klal Yisrael. The same kind of miracle happened when it seemed that the dynasty of Munkacs was coming to an end.

A son was born to the only daughter of the Minchas Eluzar on the first night of Chanukah, 1940. The Nazi jackboot was crushing Europe, and Klal Yisrael was suffering the loss of millions of *kedoshim*. The young Moshe Yehuda Leib survived and, with his parents, Harav and Rebbetzin Boruch Rabinovich and their other children, he came to Eretz Yisrael in 1944. It was a time of privation in the Holy Land, and, as penniless newcomers, Moshe Leib's family suffered more than most. Nevertheless, it was not only the Munkacser chassidim in Eretz Yisrael who rejoiced that the heritage of Munkacs had survived; even the country's foremost *gedolim* saw the hand of Hashgachah. Once, at a *bris* where Harav Rabinovich was *mohel*, the Chazon Ish asked, "Who is that child?" Told that he was the grandson of the Minchas Eluzar, the Chazon Ish said, "Bring him to me so that I can give him a *berachah*."

The Rebbe learning aleph-beis, Budapest 1944

When he was 14, Moshe Leib went to learn in the Telshe Yeshivah in Cleveland. There he won the respect and affection of the roshei hayeshivah, for his brilliant mind and intense *hasmadah*. He became especially close to Harav Mordechai Gifter, and the two had a *chavrusa* of several consecutive hours every Shabbos. Years later, Rav Gifter visited the Rebbe's yeshivah, Yeshivas Minchas Eluzar, in Brooklyn and delivered a *shiur*. He told the *bachurim* that he considered them to be his own *talmidim*, because the Rebbe himself was the rosh yeshivah's beloved *talmid*. The bond remained as long as the Rosh Yeshivah lived. The Rebbe eulogized Rav Gifter at his *levayah* held at Yeshivah Darchei Torah.

The Rebbe continuing his relationship with Telshe, with a visit to the Rosh HaYeshivah,
Harav Chaim Stein

In Telshe the future Rebbe augmented his chassidic knowledge, which was profound even at that young age, with classic "Lithuanian *lomdus.*" It was a blend that he brought with him to Bais Medrash Elyon in Monsey, after five productive years in Telshe. In Monsey, he was in his element as never before, because the yeshivah itself was the epitome of *lomdus* and Chassidus.

A major factor in molding the Rebbe was the Satmar Rav. A towering figure in the establishment of uncompromising chassidic and Torah life in America, the Satmar Rav's influence and interest spread far beyond his own growing kehillah and its many needs. When the Rebbe was still a young teenager, the Satmar Rav recognized him as the one who would reestablish the glory of Munkacs in America and beyond. The great pre-War Rav and the future post-War Rebbe had a close relationship, as the young Rebbe was molded and inspired by the universally revered Satmar Rav. The Rav's insight was prophetic. In the young adolescent, the Rav envisioned a great future leader of the next generation's Torah world. His vision was vindicated.

When Moshe Leib was in Bais Medrash Elyon, the elders of Munkacs met in Brooklyn. Led by the legendary *gabbai* of the Darkei

The Rebbe conducting a tisch as a bochur, 1959

Teshuvah and the Minchas Eluzar, Reb Chaim Ber Greenfeld, and Reb Shlomo Goldstein, another *gabbai* of the Minchas Eluzar, the participants agreed unanimously that the time had come for Munkacs to be born again, in America, and that Harav Moshe Yehuda Leib Rabinovich should be crowned as Munkacser Rav.

In 1962, the Munkacser Rebbe married the daughter of Harav Aharon Bernstein, Rosh Yeshivah of Chayei Olam in Jerusalem.

The Rebbe shortly after assuming the mantle of leadership

The Satmar Rav was *mesader kiddushin*, and he continued his close relationship with his young protégé.

One of the Rebbe's first moves after his wedding was to establish a small beis medrash and a yeshivah in Williamsburg. Following the tradition of his grandfather, he served as rosh yeshivah. From the yeshivah's first days until today, the Rebbe delivered *shiurim* and maintained a close personal contact with his *talmidim*. Although his responsibilities grew with the growth of the kehillah, his door was always open to his *talmidim*. Fundamental to his approach is that every *talmid* must be treated as an individual, so that the yeshivah will meet his needs and develop his potential. As the word spread that Munkacs had a dynamic leader in the image of his forebears, survivors and their children flocked back to their pre-War legacy.

After several years, the Rebbe moved to Boro Park, where he relocated the beis medrash and yeshivah. He established other *chinuch* institutions, primarily a cheder and mesivta for boys, girls' schools and — well aware that the long American summer vacation should not be devoid of *chinuch* — he provided summer camps. Fully aware that the world does not end in New York, the Rebbe established yeshivos, batei medrash, and kollelim in Jerusalem, Bnei Brak, Canada, and England

True to the tradition of his predecessors, the Rebbe is an exceptional scholar of Kabbalah. Indeed, many of the customs

Munkacs world headquarters in Brooklyn, New York

The Rebbe

and the *nusach hatefillah* of the Minchas Eluzar are rooted in the Kabbalah. An inkling of the Rebbe's expertise in Kabbalah can be found in his discourses and writings, but only the greatest scholars of the mysteries of the Torah fully comprehend the extent of his knowledge. The famed Jerusalem Kabbalist, Harav Asher Zelig Margolios, wrote in his *sefer Acharei Ro'i*, that he once had a difficulty in his analysis of the Kabbalistic secrets of the mitzvah of lulav, and could not find a resolution to the problem. "I asked sages here and in the Diaspora, but no one could enlighten me, until a young visitor arrived in Jerusalem, the young, wise, and holy Rav Moshe Yehuda Leib *shlita*, Admor of Munkacs and Rosh Yeshivas Minchas Eluzar, a descendant of the *Be'er Lachai Ro'i*. I asked him to look into the matter, and this is his distinguished answer." Harav Margolios goes on to quote approvingly the Rebbe's response.

In addition to his prodigious schedule of *shiurim*, personal study, and availability to people needing his blessing and guidance, the Rebbe is a prolific writer, having authored nearly a score of *sefarim* on the Talmud, Torah, and Kabbalah. He is also a talented composer. There is never a Yom Tov or family simchah that is not graced with a new composition by the Rebbe. He often says that ushering in a Yom Tov without a new *niggun* is an indication of *katnus hamochin* (small-mindedness).

In recent years the Rebbe has taken it upon himself to preserve the physical legacy of the Minchas Eluzar in Ukraine. On many occasions he traveled to Munkacs to pray, and then took it upon himself to acquire the beis medrash and home of the Minchas

The Rebbe exiting the former home of the Minchas Eluzar in Mukachevo, Ukraine, 2006

Eluzar, and succeeded in influencing the government to return the entire pre-War courtyard, including the home of the Minchas Eluzar, the succah, and the building that is now the large shul. Knowing that the city would be a magnet for large numbers of chassidim and others who revered the legacy of the holy dynasty, the Rebbe built huge *hachnasas orchim* facilities in Munkacs.

Local residents and Jews from the surrounding area can obtain kosher meals every day. Visitors can find food and lodging as needed. The former succah of the Munkacs Rebbes was transformed into a well-equipped kitchen-dining room complex for the benefit of local

The Rebbe affixing a mezuzah at the rededication of the beis medrash in Mukachevo, Ukraine, 2006

Jews and the countless visitors from around the world, who come to pray and rejuvenate themselves at the *tziunim* of the holy Rebbes of the Munkacs dynasty. In addition, the Rebbe built a beautiful *mikveh* to bring *taharas hamishpachah* back to a region that had once been fervently devout.

There are year-round programs for Yamim Tovim, and scores of Ukrainian bar mitzvah *bachurim* come to the Minchas Eluzar's beis medrash to put on tefillin for the first time. The renovation and restoration of the historic beis medrash and courtyard was marked in mid-2006 with a joyous celebration attended by throngs of chassidim from Israel, America, Australia, Canada, England, and Hungary. They came to unite themselves with the glory of the past and went home with new confidence in the future.

To come to the Munkacs *tisch* — on a yahrtzeit, a Shabbos, a Yom Tov — is to be inspired. It is an event permeated with Torah, yiras Shamayim, and unadulterated chassidic joy. The Rebbe's warmth infuses the entire assemblage. The singing, the Torah, the *shiurim*, the personally poured cup of *kos shel berachah* wine for every participant, which can take well over an hour after a long night, the *l'chaim* –

The Rebbe distributing kos shel berachah

everything is offered with love and concern for everyone, chassid or not, young or old, *talmid chacham* or layman. Everyone receives a smile and a warm *l'chaim*. The atmosphere is awesome, and people leave reluctantly, and with a sense of spiritual awe and elevation that remain with them for weeks, months — even a lifetime.

Munkacs lives and thrives. The *mesorah* of the Minchas Eluzar continues.

Chassidim pack the beis medrash during one of the Rebbe's tischen

CHAPTER 1

THE REBBE'S REASONS

In the year 5686 (1926), the Rebbe received a letter from the Jerusalem office of the Kollel of Munkacs and its Ten Suburbs. The Kollel was the recipient of the Munkacs community's charity funds to support its natives who had settled in Jerusalem and, because of the depressed economic situation in the Holy Land, needed financial assistance from abroad.

The elder of the Sephardic sages in Eretz Yisrael, Rabbi Shlomo Eliezer Elfandri, wishes to build a beis medrash and apartment to house all of the *sefarim* in his library and serve as his personal residence. After his passing, the property and its contents will be transferred to our Kollel...Other Kollelim and organizations are prevailing upon him to build this structure on their property, but he is a great zealot and does not flatter even the most prestigious of people. He has heard of Rebbe's greatness and holiness, and he therefore wishes to build the beis medrash and apartment on our Kollel's property.

[Our representatives] met with him for several hours and showed him the plan we developed. He told [the representatives] that he wishes to build the beis medrash and apartment in a high place, but they did not discuss the details with him yet. It was decided that first we have to present this idea to the Rebbe to find out if he approves.

[Rabbi Elfandri] is a great scholar, and even though he is over 100 years old, he is in full possession of his faculties. He is constantly innovating *chiddushei Torah*, and is in the process of publishing a major work of responsa. One of the powerful leaders of previous generations, he served as *Av Beis Din* in Damascus and Tzefas and now lives here in the holy city of Jerusalem.

Rabbi Elfandri was known as the Saba Kadisha, or Holy Elder, both in deference to his age and his great spiritual stature. Obviously, the leadership of the Kollel was inclined to agree to his request. The plan did not materialize, however, because the Saba Kadisha specifically wanted to build on an upper floor. The Kollel had only just begun to build Batei Machse for its members, and there were no second and third floors.

The sainted mekubal Rav Shlomo Eliezer Elfandri, the Saba Kadisha

In addition, the Kollel Munkacs property was reserved for members of the Kollel, and its by-laws did not permit it to build for anyone outside the Kollel. Nevertheless, for someone of the Saba Kadisha's stature, it would have been permitted, especially since the structure would have been left for the Kollel after his passing. However, during his lifetime, no one wanted to talk or even think about the potential gain that would be left after his passing, and so the matter was delayed and never came to fruition.

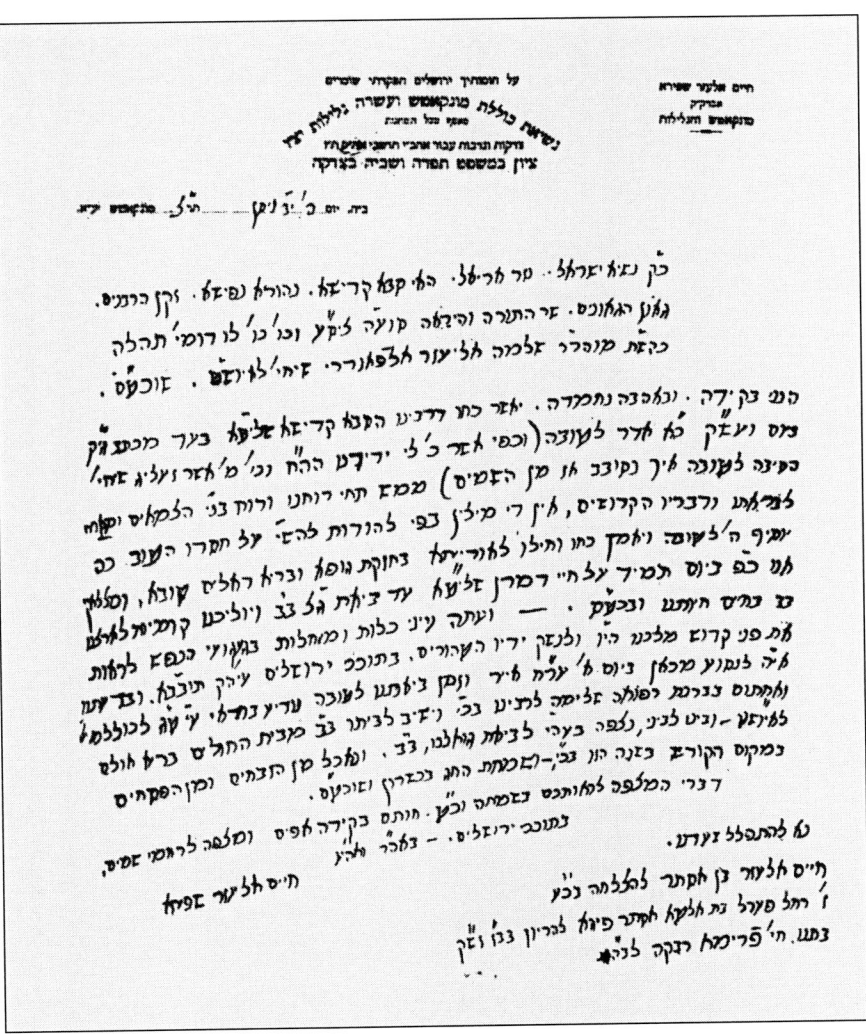

A letter written by the Minchas Eluzar to the Saba Kadisha

From the time that the Rebbe heard about the Saba Kadisha, he was on the Rebbe's mind constantly. He began to inquire about the holy man and learned of his greatness and sanctity. The Rebbe developed bonds of love to the Saba Kadisha, despite the great distance separating them, and began to speak highly of him and praise him to the people around him and in public.

The Rebbe and the Saba Kadisha started exchanging letters expressing their awe and respect for one another. Eventually, the Rebbe felt a strong yearning to see the Saba Kadisha in person. This desire, coupled with his deep love of Jerusalem, made him decide that he wished to embark on a trip to the holy city.

The following are excerpts from letters exchanged between the Rebbe and the Saba Kadisha. Only exchanges that relate to the Rebbe's desire to visit the Saba Kadisha are included.

> Wednesday, Nitzavim Vayeilech 5689, Munkacs
>
> ...I desire with all my heart and soul to see the holy countenance [of the Saba Kadisha], but I will not be able to travel after Simchas Torah because I do not wish to cause *bitul Torah* in the yeshivah where I deliver an in-depth *shiur* by being absent at the beginning of the winter *zeman*. After Chanukah, however, I can leave for a month, during which time the students can review the *shiurim*.
>
> Due to my health, I cannot travel during the hot summer months, because I cannot go outdoors in the heat of the day.
>
> [This letter was written at the time of great unrest in the Holy Land, when the Arabs of Chevron had perpetrated a bloody pogrom, and murdered nearly sixty Jews in cold blood.]
>
> In addition, my friends and chassidim have discouraged me from traveling because they were afraid of the Zionists in Jerusalem, especially after the recent destruction and bloodshed in the holy city by the Arabs. The people primarily responsible for inciting this were the Zionists and their ilk, because they accepted the Balfour (Baal Pe'or) Declaration, which will not do any good. It will only cause harm, result in destruction of our faith, and spawn jealousy among the nations, especially

the Arabs. In any event, it is a *makom sakanah*, a dangerous place.

Above all, my heart burns with a desire to see his holy countenance and speak to him for the good of the Jewish people. I cannot hold myself back any longer, especially since I heard that his honor said that he wants to see me as well. I therefore plead with my master to answer me immediately if he would agree to my coming at that time. If so, with the help of Hashem, I have faith in the blessing of the tzaddik that I will arrive safely and return safely. To me, the most important thing is that I will visit the Saba Kadisha. I am enclosing a copy of my responsa, which states my humble opinion, in keeping with the words of the Rambam, that there is no mitzvah of living in Eretz Yisrael nowadays, until Mashiach comes. One mitzvah follows another, however, and I plan to visit holy places throughout Eretz Yisrael and the graves of our holy ancestors and teachers…

Chaim Eluzar Shapira

13 Tishrei 5690

…With regard to his question, my opinion is as I stated earlier, that although it would bring me great joy to receive his presence, because the city is in distress and under pressure, it is not proper [for the Rebbe] to come now…

Shlomo Eliezer Elfandri

Tuesday, Vayechi 5690

Further to his honor's letter and response that I received after Simchas Torah: I have such a great yearning to see his honor, but we received his response that I should wait for now. My soul yearns to visit his honor, however, at least for two weeks during *Sefiras HaOmer*, after Pesach. Please do not prevent me from coming in the spring ... I await his honor's answer as soon as possible, since it takes two to three months to prepare visas.

...When my master advises me to come, I will not visit Chevron [where any Jew faced almost certain death], even if by then the storm will have quieted, for several reasons. I only want to visit Kever Rachel with a *minyan* for an hour, if his honor will agree, and to go to Meron on Lag BaOmer, along with the many others who go there. At that time the government police will be there as well. If his honor does not agree, however, I will listen to him...

Chaim Eluzar ben Esther

After writing the above letter, the Rebbe waited for an answer from the Saba Kadisha all winter. He did not receive any, however, for in the meantime, the Saba Kadisha became dangerously ill. When he recovered, he answered, in a letter dated 21 Adar 5690, "If you agree to come, come with joy." The Rebbe responded:

12 Nissan 5690

Yasher koach for the letter dated Erev Shabbos 21 Adar. (As our friend Rav Asher Zelig Margulies wrote how Heaven made it happen[1])... I have no words to thank Hashem for His kindness... May

---

1. The following is the letter from Rav Asher Zelig Margulies to which the Rebbe referered. (Rav Asher Zelig was the Saba Kadisha's assistant and the author of the *Ashrei HaIsh*, *Kumi Roni*, *Yasheiv Rucho*, and *Amudei Arazim*):

Motza'ei Shabbos Kodesh Ki Sisa, 23 Adar 5690, Jerusalem

To the Holy Rebbe:
...I am sending the Rebbe a letter written by the Saba Kadisha. This will serve the Rebbe as a *shemirah* (protection) for the trip...
[Prior to the writing of the enclosed letter,] I attempted several times to get an answer from the Saba Kadisha, at least orally, on

[the Saba Kadisha] have strength and be able to learn Torah in good health. We pray several times a day for the life of our master…

We yearn to see the holy countenance of our master and kiss his holy hands in the holy city of Jerusalem. We are planning, with Hashem's help, to travel from here on Sunday, Erev Rosh Chodesh Iyar, and we will notify of our definite arrival time with a telegram to our Kollel.

_____

the matter of the Rebbe's traveling to Eretz Yisrael, but I could not get an answer. With great difficulty he answered me, "You see that I am sick; what do you want from me?" That was the situation until last week — he was suffering indescribably. But *baruch Hashem*, since last week his condition has begun to improve, and every night since Sunday I have been awake speaking with him until midnight. Every time I brought up the subject of the Rebbe's coming to Eretz Yisrael, he put his head between his knees and came up with (trembling) as he often does…but I did not hear a clear answer from him.

On Motza'ei Purim — last Monday — I made an even stronger attempt. I brought with me all the letters that I received [from the Rebbe] during these weeks. Usually, the Saba Kadisha does not wish to have letters read to him a second time, but when I read him these letters he listened intently, answering "Amen" to each of the blessings in the letters.

…On Friday, I came to the hospital with a letter that the Rebbe had sent me express, and I read it to him. After that, a Sephardic *talmid chacham* came to visit him, and the Saba Kadisha told him, "In Munkacs there is a great Rebbe who is a true tzaddik…He fights the war of Hashem with *mesirus nefesh* and suffers tremendously, but does not flatter anyone. There is almost no one like him in this generation. I love him, and he loves me.

"Chacham Asher informed him that I am sick, and the holy tzaddik is greatly distressed by this. Who asked him [Rabbi Margulies] to tell the tzaddik and cause him pain?"

I was silent when I heard this, telling myself that it is better for me to bear the blame, because I know this holy man and I am familiar with his way of speech. After that, the visitor left.

By then, it was about half an hour to candle-lighting time, and I was debating whether to broach the subject of the Rebbe's coming with the Saba Kadisha. Suddenly, I heard him say, "Chacham Asher! Now is the time to answer the Munkacser Rebbe. Even though I have never written anything so close to the arrival of Shabbos, I do not wish to hold back good [from the Rebbe]. Give me paper and a quill." (Had I gone home to bring paper, ink, and a quill it would have already been Shabbos, but *baruch Hashem* I had had the foresight to bring a quill. I had thought that the Saba Kadisha would be unable to write, and I planned to write down what he would say.) I gave him the quill and the paper and he asked me how I knew to bring it, since he himself had not known until now that he would be writing a letter. I answered him jokingly (he enjoys hearing humor) that I am almost on the level of *ruach hakodesh,* and he joyfully said, "Quick, quick, it's almost Shabbos." He wrote and sealed the letter in front of me and told me to mail it. As soon as I left the hospital, however, I heard the sound of the shofars (as is customary in Jerusalem to blow shofars before candle-lighting). I didn't even manage to go to the *mikveh.*

Later, on Shabbos, he turned to me and asked, "Did you think that I would write a letter so close to the arrival of Shabbos? But what should I have done, I also didn't know [that I would write the letter then], but Heaven ordained that I should write it."

After the *seudah* Friday night, the Saba Kadisha asked me if I had mailed the letter. I said, "No, I didn't even go to the *mikveh.*" He spoke to me about the greatness of the Rebbe almost until midnight, and I thought to myself that on Motza'ei Shabbos I would send a telegram to Munkacs.

I close with a blessing for a speedy recovery for our master. May he return home from the hospital soon, in good health for many long years...

When the Rebbe received the Saba Kadisha's letter granting him permission to come, his joy was boundless. Immediately, he began making the many necessary preparations for the trip. Even when the Rebbe learned that the cost of the faster ship that traveled via the Trieste-Alexandria route was more than twice the price of the regular ship that traveled via the Trieste-Jaffa route, he was not deterred. He hurried to take the faster ship so that he could arrive as quickly as possible. Many people prevailed upon him to delay his departure until after Shavuos, when many of his chassidim were going to be traveling, but the Rebbe did not wish to delay his trip at all. Even so, a very respectable group joined him on his journey.

In the morning, he told me that until that day he had not left his bed, but that today he wanted a *minyan* to come to the hospital to daven. He said that he would leave his bed to have an *aliyah* to the Torah and I was very happy...

After Havdalah I prepared the telegram: "The Saba is better and he wrote that the Rebbe should come in joy."

...The Saba Kadisha was very happy that the tzaddik had prayed on his behalf, and he thanked him a thousand times for this...

May [the Rebbe] have a successful trip and may Hashem watch him along the way...

Yeshaya Asher Zelig Margulies

CHAPTER 2

THE TRIP

O n Sunday, Erev Rosh Chodesh Iyar, the Rebbe addressed the students of the yeshivah, citing the halachah (*Yoreh Deah* 270:1) that one is obligated to sell a *Sefer Torah* for the sake of the mitzvah of *pidyon shevuyim* (redemption of captives). "Do not think it strange," he told the students, "that I am leaving you now, at the beginning of the *zeman*, to go to Eretz Yisrael, even though this will cause *bitul Torah* for you for a month. In this case, *bitul Torah* is actually the validation of Torah." The Rebbe added that his trip was intended to bring about *pidyon shevuyim* for all of Klal Yisrael, and that the students should continue learning Torah diligently during his absence. He did not explain why he considered it to be *pidyon shevuyim*. Apparently he felt that his meeting with the great tzaddik would have enormous spiritual ramifications.

The following day, Monday, we boarded a train to Vienna. Our departure from the people of Munkacs — and from chassidim all along the way as we traveled — was with tremendous pomp and honor to the Rebbe. When the Rebbe saw all this honor, he said, "Master of the Universe, it is known and revealed before You that I am not doing this for the honor of my father's house, but in order to greet the tzaddik of the generation in Jerusalem."

We arrived in Vienna the next day, Tuesday, and began working on obtaining travel permits from the Egyptian consul. On Wednesday night, we again boarded the train and traveled through Austria, Yugoslavia, and Italy.

Finally, we arrived in the port city of Trieste on Thursday morning. All that day and the next we tried to obtain a travel permit for the Rebbe's son-in-law, Rav Baruch. All we needed was a transit visa that would allow him to travel from Alexandria to Eretz Yisrael. The rest of us had already managed to obtain visas, but he was a Polish citizen, and the Egyptian consuls in Vienna and Trieste would not give permission for a Polish citizen to pass through Egyptian borders. Despite our efforts, which included the intervention of high-ranking officials, we could not procure the necessary permit. This caused the Rebbe tremendous distress, to the point where he debated whether the whole trip was worthwhile if his beloved son-in-law could not accompany him.

The SS Vienna, which carried the Rebbe and his entourage from Trieste to Alexandria

Late Friday afternoon, we brought all our belongings to the port and boarded the *SS Vienna*, a large, high-speed ship traveling from Trieste to Alexandria. We settled ourselves on the ship, donned Shabbos clothing, lit candles and accepted Shabbos upon ourselves early (as per the halachah of setting out on a maritime voyage; *Orach Chaim* 248:1).

We brought all of the Shabbos food with us onto the ship, and the ship's officers gave us a large room in which to daven and hold our *seudah*. At the time, we were the only passengers on the ship; the other passengers did not board until the following day, when the ship was scheduled to leave. Many Jews from Trieste boarded the ship while it was docked to hear the Friday night and Shabbos morning davening. As for us, we barely sensed that we were on a ship and not in Munkacs.

On Shabbos morning, we davened early so that we could finish before midday, when the remainder of the passengers would board. Around boarding time, the Jews of Trieste took leave of us and gave us their blessings.

Before the ship's departure, the manager of the company that owned the *Vienna* brought the ship's captain to the Rebbe and instructed him to do whatever the Rebbe wished during the entire journey, and to behave toward the Rebbe and his entourage with the appropriate respect. The manager also pledged to use his contacts in Alexandria to procure a travel permit for the Rebbe's son-in-law, but he could not guarantee that he would be successful, so Rav Baruch had no choice but to leave the ship and stay in Trieste. He was joined by one other person, who accompanied him several days later on a ship that traveled directly from Trieste to Jaffa. We were sorely disappointed that he was not with us.

The beginning of the trip was uneventful, and we spent a peaceful Shabbos and Motza'ei Shabbos on board. On Sunday, however, the weather changed, and the waves became much more powerful.

Sunday afternoon, the Rebbe left his room to go up to the deck of the ship, and the entire group followed him. We davened Minchah and then Maariv on the deck, and then we began to feel sick from the rocking of the ship and the strength of the waves. Nevertheless,

The Rebbe (far left) in conversation on the ship

we recited *Kiddush Levanah* joyously, hoping that the sea would settle. That night, we felt the rocking of the ship intensely, and the sound of the wind and the waves resonated in our ears.

On Monday morning, we had a close brush with death. The steamship *Orient* entered the waters where our ship was traveling. The sailors on the *Vienna* blew trumpets loudly on the upper deck to warn the *Orient*, but her sailors did not hear the sounds at all. Our captain quickly turned the *Vienna* slightly, averting a potentially di-

Members of the Rebbe's entourage aboard the ship

sastrous collision. Later, the ship's officers informed us that we had experienced a great miracle.

At the time, the Rebbe was wearing his tefillin. When he found out what had happened, he thanked Hashem for His kindness, and referred to the merit of his ancestors, especially his holy grandfather, Rav Moshe Leib of Sassov. After Shacharis, he drank a *l'chaim* with those present to commemorate the miracle. All this happened between the time the Rebbe donned his Rashi and Rabbeinu Tam tefillin.

Later, the Rebbe recalled that the previous night we had performed *Kiddush Levanah,* even though seven full days had not passed since the appearance of the new moon. The Rebbe had a tradition from his forefathers to perform *Kiddush Levanah* only after the seventh day of the month, but for some reason none of us had realized that it was not yet the optimal time for the mitzvah. The Rebbe declared that Heaven had ordained that we should perform *Kiddush Levanah* earlier than usual so that the merit of the mitzvah should protect us.

That night, while the sea was still stormy, the Rebbe began planning his itinerary in Eretz Yisrael. He said that if possible, he wished to visit the tombs of kings of the Davidic dynasty before visiting any other holy place. What is more fitting to visit first, he said, than the grave of David HaMelech? (At the end, however, this plan did not materialize, because the keys to the tombs of the Davidic kings on Mount Zion were in the hands of the Arabs, and it was not possible to have the tombs opened on the first or second day of our visit, only later.)

The sea was stormy all that night and the next day, rocking the ship violently and tossing us around. By this time, we understood well the meaning of the Gemara that says, "Eretz Yisrael is acquired with suffering" (*Berachos* 5a). It was almost impossible for us to stand without grabbing hold of something, and we begged Hashem to save us from the merciless sea.

The Rebbe davened *Shemoneh Esrei* of Shacharis sitting down, so that he could have *kavanah*. He davened fervently, invoking the merit of

Members of the Rebbe's entourage aboard the ship

Members of the Rebbe's entourage in Egypt.
The Duna-Szerdahely Rebbe is on the right. Next to him is the Turda Rebbe.

the tzaddik whom we were planning to visit and the merit of the Holy Land. Eventually, the storm started to subside, and the knowledge that we were getting close to our destination revived our spirits.

That afternoon, after three days on the ship, we were finally able to see the city of Alexandria ahead of us, and we thanked Hashem for bringing us to that point.

On the shore were three people dressed in white, as was the custom of those living in Jerusalem. These individuals had traveled almost twenty-four hours from Jerusalem to Alexandria to greet the Rebbe. This heartwarming sight aroused within us a deep feeling of love for the Holy City and its people.

We had no trouble from the border inspectors, who merely looked at one or two of the many pieces of luggage with us. This was thanks to the efforts of the Sephardic magnate David Eliyahu, the son of Ezra Anzarat of Alexandria. David Eliyahu had received a letter with instructions from the Saba Kadisha to welcome us. (The Saba Kadisha had served earlier as a rav in Damascus, where David Eliyahu had lived, and he had become one of the Saba Kadisha's followers.) He met us at the port with his automobile, and graciously brought us to his father's palatial residence. We stayed for a day until we continued our journey to Eretz Yisrael by train.

Tuesday night, we went to the "Shaarei Tefillah" shul in Alexandria to daven. We heard the Sephardic Jews davening Maariv, and their pronunciation was completely foreign to us. After they finished, they made room for us to conduct our own *minyan* in our own *nusach*, and they were equally mystified by the way we davened. Nevertheless, they were moved, and they kissed the Rebbe's hands reverently and wished him a safe trip.

We were bewildered by the davening and customs of the Jews of Alexandria, but the Rebbe defended them. "Who is like Your people, Yisrael," he said, adding that Hashem has children serving Him in every country and in every city across the world.

Wednesday afternoon, we boarded a train traveling to Eretz Yisrael via Benha-Kantara-Lod. Benha-Kantara is at the border between Egypt and Eretz Yisrael, and that is where we crossed the Suez Canal and entered the territory of Eretz Yisrael. After undergoing passport inspection, we again boarded the train in Eretz Yisrael. To us, however, the place seemed as foreign as the gentile territory we had previously passed through. The officials we saw were Jewish, our brothers, yet we were alienated from them. These were secular Zionists talking modern Hebrew — a distorted version of the holy tongue of our Torah and Gemara. We saw these types of people on the train and at every stop along the way.

The train traveled through the desert where our ancestors had traveled on their way from Egypt to Eretz Yisrael. It is said that from where we were, it is possible to see Mount Sinai, where the Torah was given, but we could not see anything because we were traveling in the dark. As the train rolled on toward its destination, we sensed that we were getting closer to the palace of the King, and it was a very exciting night for us.

Now, I will detail the events of the thirteen days that we spent in the Holy Land.

CHAPTER 3

THE FIRST DAY

Thursday morning found us in the blessed land of Eretz Yisrael. As the train traveled through the Holy Land, we were excited and awed to hear the names of the railway stops being called out — Yavneh, Beitar, and other holy places mentioned in Tanach and Gemara.

We reached the city of Lod, where we had to transfer to a different train. That was where we merited to step onto the holy soil of Eretz Yisrael, and that was where prestigious people from Jerusalem — Sephardic, Ashkenazic, and chassidic — began coming to greet the Rebbe. The crowd was led by a tall, elderly, impressive-looking man. When we asked who he was, we were told that he was the great *gaon*, Harav Chaim Shaul HaKohen Dweck, author of *Eiphah Sheleimah* and other *sefarim*, who learned in Yeshivah Rechovos HaNahar in Jerusalem, a yeshivah for *mekubalim*. Even though he was blind, he and all of the scholars in the yeshivah came to greet the Rebbe in Lod, for he was greatly impressed by the trouble the Rebbe had taken to come to Eretz Yisrael.

The mekubal, Rav Chaim Shaul HaKohen Dweck (right), at the kabbalas panim for the Rebbe at Lod

Rav Yaakov Chaim Sofer,
author of Kaf HaChaim

Rav Shalom Yosef HaLevi Alshich

Rabbi Yaakov Chaim Sofer, head of the Persian community and author of the *Kaf HaChaim*, and Rabbi Shalom Yosef HaLevi Alshich, leader of the Yemenite community in Jerusalem, also came to greet us, as did many other prominent individuals.

The Rebbe shed tears as he asked them why they had troubled themselves for his sake. "I came to greet you in Jerusalem and listen to your Torah learning and your wisdom of Kabbalah," he said.

Harav Dweck answered him, "The reason I came here to greet [the Rebbe] was for the sake of honoring the Torah. This is especially so for a tzaddik ben tzaddik like [the Rebbe], who is the son of the holy *mekubal*, the author of *Be'er Lachai Ro'i* and *Darkei Teshuvah*."

At that point, a messenger delivered a letter of blessing from the Saba Kadisha:

> 10 Iyar 5690
>
> ...Today is a day of good news. I was delighted when they told me that the land has been illuminated by his honor...Blessed is he who comes in the Name of Hashem...it would have been appropriate to greet [the Rebbe] immediately, for I am love-sick, and I should run to the man of G-d, but I am unable to go out. May Hashem in His mercy send me a full recovery, and may [the Rebbe's] coming here be a favorable omen for the redemption of the Jewish people...
> Shlomo Eliezer Elfandri

Letters of blessing also arrived from a number of tzedakah organizations, kollelim, and yeshivos in the Holy City of Yerushalayim.

At later train stops along the way, other people greeted us, among them many prestigious individuals dressed in white Shabbos clothing. They welcomed the Rebbe joyously, with song, but the Rebbe stopped them. "We are obligated to tear our clothing when we see holy cities in their state of destruction; so how can we sing now, when Mashiach has not yet come?"

On the way from Lod to Jerusalem, the train was packed with the many people who had come to greet us.

בס"ד

חכם הרזים בא לעיר

ביום חמישי י' אייר כ"ה לעומר בשעה 1 (לשא"י) יגיע נחמתנו בית ה' נתיבי ירושלם ת"ו

אדמו"ר הגאון הקדוש צדיק יסוד עולם מרבה לשכינה מקובל אלקי שר בית הזוהר נכש"ת

רבינו **חיים אלעזר שפירא** שליט"א

בן הגה"צ אדמו"ר איש האלקים בעל דרכי תשובה זצ"ל
אבדק"ק מונקאטש יצ"ו

והנני מודיע בשער בת רבים שחוב קדוש מוטל ע"כ חכמי ירושלם ובראשם חברינו לומדי חכמת האמת ויודעי ח"ן
ליתן כבוד לתורה לילך לתחנת הרכבת לקבל פני השכינה פני קודש הקדשים רבינו שליט"א הנ"ל ·

חיים שאול דוויך הכהן

ר"ם דישיבת המכונים "רחובות הנהר"

Proclamation of Rav Dweck calling on Jerusalemites to welcome the Rebbe

We davened Shacharis and read from the Torah. The Rebbe had the first *aliyah*, in place of a Kohen, and he *bentched gomel* for having safely crossed the sea. Afterward, whiskey and food were distributed, and everyone made a joyous *l'chaim*.

The *talmidei chachamim* of Jerusalem argued over where the Rebbe should stay, each vying for the privilege of hosting him. When the Rebbe said that he would ask the advice of the Saba Kadisha about where to stay, one person objected, "But the Saba Kadisha does not live in the Old City of Jerusalem and is unfamiliar with its streets."

To this, the Rebbe replied, "The Saba Kadisha is familiar with the pathways of the heavenly city of Jerusalem, and he therefore knows the earthly Jerusalem very well."

JERUSALEM AND THE KOSEL HAMAARAVI

Our first reaction when we arrived in the Holy City of Jerusalem was one of joy, especially since we were greeted by masses of people rejoicing at our arrival. But before we even stepped foot on the ground, we saw that tears were streaming from the Rebbe's eyes. He immediately tore his garment in a way that could not be repaired, crying brokenheartedly. We all tore our clothing and said the *pesukim* of *Tzidduk HaDin* (Acceptance of God's Judgment) as dictated by halachah.

There were so many people who had come to greet the Rebbe that it was impossible for him to make his way through the crowds. He remained standing at the window in the train wearing the special hat that he wore on Rosh Chodesh and other special occasions, and extended his hand outside the train with a smile to give *Shalom Aleichem*. Eventually, he descended from the train.

We made our way toward the gates of Jerusalem, and with much effort and with the help of the police we passed through the crowds together with the Rebbe.

From the train station, we traveled by automobile directly to the holy Kosel HaMaaravi. On the way, we gazed at the city of Jerusalem, but we could not pay full attention to the details of the Holy City, for our hearts ached when we remembered Tzion of old. We saw the tears rolling down the Rebbe's face, and as we got closer to the site of the Holy of Holies, he turned pale and began to moan and groan.

Panoramic view of Jerusalem

Yidden awaiting the Rebbe's arrival at the train station in Jerusalem

We were gripped by fear and awe as we approached via Mount Zion on the narrow path, accessible only by foot, leading up to the Temple Mount. With tremulous footsteps we tread on the holy stones, accompanied by a large crowd. Finally, we saw the beautiful Kosel, the remnant of the wall around the Temple Mount from where the *Shechinah* has never departed

The Rebbe removed his shoes and tore his clothes again, as dictated by halachah. He approached the Kosel lovingly, stooped over, sobbing, as a child toward its mother.

When the Rebbe began reciting Tehillim (Psalm 79) — "A psalm by Asaph: O G-d, nations have entered into Your inheritance, they have defiled Your Sanctuary…" — even a heart of stone would have melted. The people present tearfully repeated it after him. It was vastly different saying those verses at the site of the Beis HaMikdash than saying them in another part of the world. Here, we saw in front of our own eyes how the nations had defiled the Sanctuary. To us, it seemed as though the destruction had just now occurred.

We recited Psalm 137, "By the rivers of Babylon, there we sat and also wept when we remembered Zion," as well as other chapters of Tehillim, the Rebbe pouring his heart out before Hashem.

The Kosel HaMaaravi

To those who live in the Diaspora and have not experienced the holiness of Eretz Yisrael and Jerusalem, it is impossible to describe how one feels upon seeing the Kosel HaMaaravi — the awe, the excitement, the fear of Hashem whose *Shechinah* rested in the edifice behind that wall. It is the holiest of all places, the gate of heaven, the site of *Akeidas Yitzchak*, the place where Yaakov Avinu rested, the location of the two Batei Mikdash where the Jews brought sacrifices and the Kohanim performed their service reverently, and the place where the third Beis HaMikdash will be built.

But its present state is deplorable, for the Ishmaelites have built an abomination upon that holy site. Before our eyes, the gentiles do there as they please, and there is nothing we can do until Hashem decides to bring the redemption.

It is no surprise that a Jew who traveled hundreds of miles on land and sea is heartbroken when he comes to the Kosel. There, a Jewish soul longs for Hashem's closeness in a way that simply cannot be experienced outside Eretz Yisrael. The holiness of the place causes every person to feel the pain of the holy *Shechinah* and the pain of the Jewish people — some people more, some people less, according to their level.

Our holy master, the Rebbe's father, also greatly desired to visit Jerusalem and other cities in Eretz Yisrael. He especially wanted to visit the grave of Rabbi Shimon bar Yochai in Meron. He felt, however, that if he would go to Eretz Yisrael and see the Temple Mount and the Kosel in their destruction, he would not be able go on living. There were still *sefarim* that he needed to complete for the benefit of the world, and he was therefore afraid to visit Eretz Yisrael. (Going to Eretz Yisrael only to visit Tzefas and Meron on Lag BaOmer was not an option, for he felt that it would be disrespectful to travel to the Holy Land and not visit Jerusalem.) He therefore decided that it was better to remain where he was.

A discerning eye noticed something of a similar phenomenon with the Rebbe. When he took leave of the Kosel after davening and pouring his heart out and kissing the holy stones, it was an effort for him to lift his feet. But the knowledge that he was going from the Kosel straight to see the Saba Kadisha calmed his soul, for he hoped that the redemption would come sooner because of the Saba Kadisha.

The Rebbe with chassidim in Jerusalem

THE SABA KADISHA

When we left the Kosel, the streets were full of people, and we once again needed the help of the police to make way for the tzaddik to pass. Then, we entered the automobile that would take us out of the Old City to the "Ruchamah" neighborhood where the Saba Kadisha lived.

When we arrived at the house of the Saba Kadisha, we saw that a huge crowd had gathered to observe the meeting of the two tzaddikim. The door of the small house opened, and we saw a giant of a man, his head a bit stooped, thin, frail bones jutting out from his skin, his face long and not wide, large, sunken eyes — like the gemstones *odem, pit'dah,* and *barekes* — with full eyebrows surrounding them, his beard grown short and with small white hairs, his *peyos* gathered around his face and protruding from his temples like snow, his hair neither bushy nor thin. He was wearing silken Shabbos clothing and a red hat with a tassel (called a fez), as the Sephardim and their leaders customarily wear. His appearance cast fear on all who saw him, especially those who had never seen him before. He was about 120 years old, but his strength had not waned.

The home of the Saba Kadisha

The Saba Kadisha stood and waited to joyously greet the honored guest, and the Rebbe hurried to enter. The Rebbe shook the Saba Kadisha's hand submissively, and the Saba Kadisha returned the gesture. The Rebbe wished to kiss the Saba Kadisha's hands, but the Saba Kadisha did not allow him to do so. The Rebbe begged him, "Please, let us kiss the hands of [our master]," but he answered, "Heaven forbid for a great person like [the Rebbe]."

"Before our master, I am like a student before his rebbi," the Rebbe said tearfully.

"*Chalilah,*" the Saba Kadisha replied.

After that, the Saba Kadisha sat down on a long bench and seated the Rebbe adjacent to him, on the bench. The two sat together and delighted in mutual love. Anyone who did not see their joy has never in his life seen the joy of tzaddikim meeting one another. Tears of happiness streamed from the Rebbe's eyes, and he made the *berachah* of *Shehecheyanu* in a ringing voice. All those present answered "Amen," moved by the sight.

In a display of honor for the Rebbe, the Saba Kadisha extended his holy hand to shake the hands of all of the rabbanim of the Rebbe's entourage and to us as well. Normally, the Saba Kadisha did not shake the hand of any person, even prominent individuals; he would wish them "Shalom" only with his holy mouth. He had hidden reasons for this practice, but he nevertheless made an exception on this occasion.

The Saba Kadisha instructed the people of his house to honor the Rebbe with the fruits of Eretz Yisrael and with beverages. The Rebbe made a *l'chaim*, expressing the wish that we should merit, together with our teacher the Saba Kadisha, to greet Mashiach and to bring the sacrifices of the upcoming holiday of Shavuos in the Beis HaMikdash. The Saba Kadisha answered "Amen" and told the Rebbe that they would yet discuss this matter further.

The atmosphere in the house was so joyous that the people present burst out in song, and the two tzaddikim started to cry out of happiness. These moments are inscribed upon our hearts eternally.

The conversation continued, and the Rebbe told the Saba Kadisha about the events that had transpired during the trip. He told him of the narrow escape from death on the ship, describing how he had davened then that we be saved in the merit of the Saba Kadisha whom we were planning to visit in Jerusalem. The Saba Kadisha answered, "Good, good."

The Rebbe then expressed to the Saba Kadisha his distress over the fact that his son-in-law had remained behind, and he asked him to daven that his son-in-law should arrive safely at his destination. The Saba Kadisha responded encouragingly to this as well.

The Rebbe also gave the Saba Kadisha a *kvittel* with his name and the names of his family, and the tzaddik accepted the *kvittel* with love and friendship.

The Saba Kadisha asked the Rebbe how long he planned to stay in Eretz Yisrael, and the Rebbe answered that he wished to stay about two weeks. He added that he planned to spend Lag BaOmer in Meron, but that he wished to be back in Munkacs for Shavuos, not in Eretz Yisrael while it was still in its destruction.

The Rebbe explained that he did not want to forfeit the holiness of the second day of Yom Tov, which according to the early Kabbalists is greater than that of the first day. He added that he did not wish to contravene the opinion of the author of the *Chacham Tzvi*, who wrote (Responsum 167) that residents of the Diaspora who visit

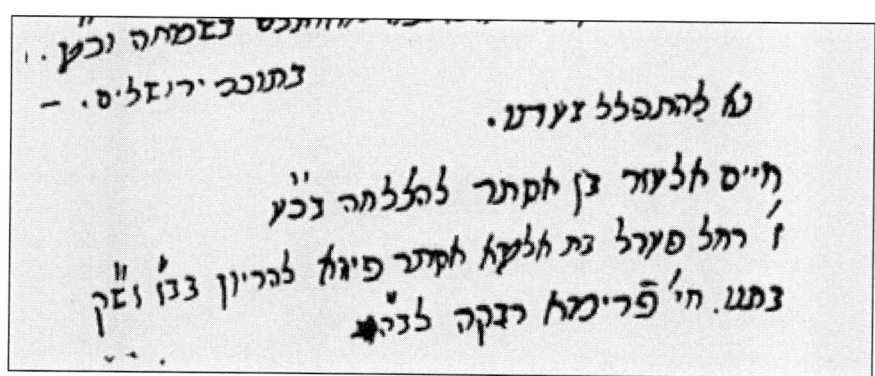

A kvittel that the Rebbe sent to the Saba Kadisha in one of his letters

Eretz Yisrael temporarily have the same halachah as residents of Eretz Yisrael and should not keep the second day of Yom Tov during their stay. To follow that ruling, however, was very difficult for the Rebbe to do, since it is not the accepted practice.

The Saba Kadisha accepted his words graciously.

When the Rebbe left the home of the Saba Kadisha, he told us that his prior impression of the tzaddik had not been mistaken. From the time he had heard about the greatness of the Saba Kadisha several years earlier, he had longed to see him. Now that he had seen him, he was greatly awed by him.

RABBI YOSEF CHAIM SONNENFELD

From there, we went directly back to the Old City to visit the holy tzaddik, Rabbi Yosef Chaim Sonnenfeld, the leader of the Ashkenazi community of Jerusalem. At the time, Rabbi Sonnenfeld was ill, and sent people to inform the Rebbe that because of his illness he could not come out to greet him.

There were many people waiting to receive the Rebbe at Rabbi Sonnenfeld's house. The elderly rav mustered all of his strength to stand up, and he received the distinguished guest with great joy. Tearfully, he recited the blessing of *Shehecheyanu*. He then blessed the Rebbe that just as he had merited seeing Jerusalem in its destruction, so may he merit seeing it rebuilt, speedily. The Rebbe was served a variety of refreshments and beverages, from which he distributed *shirayim* to everyone in the house. After that, the two tzaddikim exchanged *divrei Torah*, and then they parted.

Rabbi Sonnenfeld escorted the Rebbe outside his house, in deference to his honor. He wished to escort him further, but the Rebbe insisted that he refrain due to his weakness and age.

The Rebbe told Rabbi Sonnenfeld the story of the two great tzaddikim, Rabbi Yitzchak Isaac of Kaliv and Rabbi Moshe Teitelbaum of Uheli, who went together to the inauguration of the shul in the community of Nanosch. When they arrived at the door of the shul, each one wanted to show honor to the other, and refused to enter first. After arguing over this for a while, the Rebbe of Uheli told the Rebbe of Kaliv to enter first. "If I am not as great as you, you should enter first because of your superior greatness. And if I am greater

Rav Yosef Chaim Sonnenfeld (second from left), the Av Beis Din of Jerusalem

than you, I am commanding you to go first and you have to listen to me." Thus, the Rebbe of Kaliv had no choice but to enter first.

With this story, the Rebbe convinced Rabbi Sonnenfeld to return to his house and not exert himself.

LODGINGS

We traveled to the new city of Jerusalem, entering the neighborhood of Kollel Munkacs, where the Rebbe was going to stay in the home of the scholar Rabbi Chanoch Chaim HaKohen. As in all the places we visited with the Rebbe, the neighborhood was full of men, women, and children who had come to see him. We were deeply moved when we heard that even the devout women of Jerusalem, upon seeing the Rebbe pass, whispered to one another, "A holy man is passing — may he merit to greet Mashiach, and may his coming be a sign of blessing and redemption." These were not people who lived with luxuries; their lives were lives of suffering like most of those living in Eretz Yisrael, yet they dedicated themselves to Hashem, anxiously awaiting the redemption. Who is like Your people, Yisrael. In the merit of righteous women they are worthy of being redeemed.

Rav Chanoch Chaim HaKohen, the Rebbe's host in Batei Munkacs, Jerusalem

We davened Minchah and Maariv in the "Tiferes Tzvi" shul of Kollel Munkacs, near where we were staying. The davening was no different from what we were accustomed to, except for the recitation of *Borchu* before *Aleinu* and the omission of *Baruch Hashem L'olam* in Maariv. The Rebbe davened in that shul, along with a large gathering of people, each day that we were in Jerusalem.

One of the buildings in the Munkacs Kollel complex

The huge crowds that descended upon the Rebbe in Jerusalem, to hear his wisdom and his opinions on matters relating to Eretz Yisrael and other issues, necessitated the posting of signs stating that no one was

The Tiferes Tzvi shul in Batei Munkacs, Jerusalem

allowed to enter his holy presence and speak to him without receiving authorization from a special committee. The purpose of the Rebbe's stay was only to visit holy places, not to be bothered by trivial conversation.

CHAPTER 4

THE SECOND DAY

THE YEMENITE JEWS

Friday, Erev Shabbos, was the second day of our stay in Jerusalem. Earlier, the Rebbe had expressed a desire to observe the customs of Yemenite Jews in Jerusalem at a *bris milah*, and Friday morning, he was told that in the Yemenite shul in the neighborhood known as Machanayim there would be a *bris* around midday.

We went there at about 11 a.m., and we were told us that we would have to wait about another half hour. When the Rebbe asked why they do not do the mitzvah early in the morning, they answered that in the morning the people of the shul go to work, so they preferred to wait until midday, when everyone could gather together.

In the meantime, we decided to visit the caves of the Sanhedrin, which were located not far away on a mountain in the northern part of Jerusalem. We climbed mountains and descended into valleys un-

A Yemenite cheder in Jerusalem

til we arrived at the cave where the members of the Great Sanhedrin are buried. With trepidation, we passed through the opening at the base of the mountain, entering first into one cave, then into another. We lit candles and saw several seemingly hollow crypts, both large and small. We were amazed by this sight.

The Rebbe pledged to give tzedakah in the merit of the souls of the tzaddikim buried there, and davened a short prayer for Klal Yisrael and for the redemption.

From there, we returned to the shul in Machanayim. The Yemenite Jews wished to honor the Rebbe by having him serve as *sandak* and say the blessings, but he refused; he wanted to observe their customs from beginning to end.

The men, women, and children of the congregation were already there, as was their leader (the *"Chacham"*). Some of the children were barefoot, wearing worn, tattered clothing, but there was a certain purity upon their faces.

The father came in with the baby and began leading those present in a circle around the table. They walked around joyously, singing *Ana B'choach* and sweetly reciting the verses *Hashem melech, Shema Yisrael, Ana Hashem hoshiyah na,* and others. We were all deeply moved by the sight.

The *bris* was performed, and the cup of wine was given to the *Chacham*. After the usual blessings (*Asher kidash yedid mibeten* and *Borei pri hagafen*), a blessing was made over *besamim*, and fragrant branches were distributed to everyone to smell.

The baby was named after his father. This practice is permitted by Yemenite custom, but was a marvel to us. After delicacies were distributed to all those present, we left, accompanied by the congregants, who kissed the hands of the Rebbe and leaned over, touching their heads to his hand, as a *segulah* and display of honor to the great man. (The custom of the Sephardic and Yemenite Jews of Eretz Yisrael is to bend their head and touch it to the hand of a great person, just as we put our hand on a *mezuzah*, a *Sefer Torah*, or other holy object, and then kiss our hand.)

THE GRAVE OF SHIMON HATZADDIK

From there we traveled straight to the grave of the holy Tanna and Kohen Gadol, Shimon HaTzaddik, one of the last remaining members of the Great Assembly, who lived at the beginning of the Second Temple era. On his yahrtzeit, the 29th day of Tishrei, the people of Jerusalem traditionally gather at his grave.

When we entered the tomb built above the cave where he is buried, we began to tremble at the thought of the great man before whom we were standing. The outline of his grave is visible at the entrance to the cave, and the hidden crypt is hewn into the mountain.

We said some Tehillim there, and we davened with the fervent desire that the Kohen Gadol should offer our prayers on the altar of Heaven in the merit of the prayers of the Rebbe.

We left and made our way to the nearby tombs of the Minor Sanhedrins [Sanhedrei Ketanah]. Since it was Erev Shabbos, however, there was a lot left to do, and we could not spend time there; all we could do was look at the crypts from afar. The Rebbe focused his thoughts and his lips moved slightly.

HAR HAZEISIM

Next, we traveled to Har Hazeisim, the great mountain about which it is said (*Zechariah* 14:4), "[G-d's] feet will stand on that day on Har Hazeisim." From there, we were able to see from afar the ruins where the Holy of Holies in the Beis HaMikdash used to be. When the Rebbe saw this, he cried and averted his eyes, unable to bear the sight of gentiles defiling the Sanctuary.

Har Hazeisim, the cemetery where Jerusalem's dead are buried, is also the historic burial place of many Torah giants and great Rabbis of previous generations. The graves are spread over the entire area of the mountain, and it is impossible to discern exactly where they are. Anyone who walks on the mountain to visit a marked grave has no idea which other holy graves he may be trampling on. This knowledge makes it frightening to walk on Har Hazeisim, but there is no choice — it is impossible to visit any grave there otherwise, and the honor of the dead is not diminished by our unintentional oversights, especially since we cannot know if we are indeed walking on graves.

The first grave we came to on Har Hazeisim was that of the prophet Zechariah, who is buried inside a dome with a circular tower built around it. The Rebbe rested his hands and head on the wall of the dome and prayed briefly. The rest of us davened briefly as well, fearful of standing before the Kohen and prophet and opening our mouths before him.[1]

---

1. The Rebbe said that when Rabbi Eluzar Mendel, son of Rabbi Moshe of Lelov, used to go to Har Hazeisim to daven at his father's grave, he would also visit the grave of the prophet Zechariah, but only for a short while. The reason for the short duration of his visits was that he was afraid to arouse heavenly anger over the murder of Zechariah, as the verse states, "Should Kohen and prophet be slain in the Sanctuary of the L-rd?" (*Eichah* 2:20).

Kever of the prophet Zechariah on Har Hazeisim in Jerusalem

Not far from the grave of Zechariah is the grave of the holy tzaddik Rabbi Moshe of Lelov, the son of the Rebbe Dovid of Lelov and the son-in-law of the Yid HaKadosh of P'shis'cha. Rabbi Moshe of Lelov spent 74 days in Eretz Yisrael, the same number as the years he lived, and during those days he made intensive preparations to visit the Kosel HaMaaravi. He did not manage to go to the Kosel even once, however, for circumstances prevented him from doing so, and he was deeply pained that Heaven did not allow him to realize his wish of visiting that holy site.

After that, we came to the holy grave of the Ohr HaChaim HaKadosh. Originally from Sali, the Ohr HaChaim arrived in Eretz Yisrael at the end of the year 5502 (1742), and passed away on the 15th of Tammuz the following summer at the age of 47. Near the Ohr HaChaim are buried his two wives, great women of noted achievements.

The Rebbe bent over the grave and poured his heart out to Hashem, saying Tehillim and davening tearfully. All those standing around him were deeply moved. Then, he learned a selection of the Ohr HaChaim's commentary on the Chumash.

The Rebbe related a story he had heard from his holy ancestors that demonstrated the greatness and holiness of the Ohr HaChaim. Once, one of the people close to the tzaddik came to him crying bitter tears and poured out his heart. Previously, this man had earned a respectable livelihood, but his fortunes had suddenly taken a turn for the worse. He told the Ohr HaChaim that his family was poverty-stricken and did not have even bread to eat, and begged the tzaddik to daven for him and assure him that his situation would improve.

The Ohr HaChaim took pity on the man. He wrote a note on parchment, folded it up tightly and gave it to the pauper, instructing him to hold onto the note tightly and to take it directly to the Kosel. "Find a space between the holy stones and put the note there," the Ohr HaChaim said. "Then go home and you will be saved."

The man left holding the note. On his way, it became very windy outside. His upper hat blew off, but he paid no attention. He held onto his lower hat with his left hand and held the note in his right. But the wind blew off his lower hat as well, leaving him bareheaded. As he tried to retrieve his hat in the fierce wind, the note fell out of his hand and blew away. Bitterly disappointed, he went back to the house of the Ohr HaChaim and told him what had happened.

"What shall I do for you, then?" the Ohr HaChaim responded. "It was not meant to be."

Later, the note was found in the streets of Jerusalem, signed "Chaim ben Attar." People brought it back to the Ohr HaChaim, and they saw then that it was addressed to the *Shechinah*, using these words: "My sister, my love, my dove, my perfection (see *Shir HaShirim* 5:2), I ask that You mercifully bestow good livelihood on So-and-so."

From this story, one can understand a bit of the holiness of the Ohr HaChaim.

From there, we went to the grave of the holy Kabbalist, Rabbi Shalom Sharabi (the Rashash) and his son Rabbi Chizkiyah Yitzchak. Above the grave of the Rashash is the grave of Rabbi Yom Tov Elgazi. We also visited the grave of Rabbi Yisrael Yaakov Elgazi, the father of Rabbi Yom Tov Elgazi and the author of *Ar'ah D'Rabbanan*, as well as the grave of Rabbi Chizkiyah di Silva, author of the *Pri Chadash*. Rabbi Chizkiyah's wife is buried on his right, and they share a single tombstone. At all of these gravesites we poured out

Kever of Rav Yisrael Yaakov Elgazi and his son Rav Yom Tov Elgazi, on Har Hazeisim

our hearts, hoping that our prayers would be accepted by Heaven in the merit of the holy tzaddikim, may they protect us and be favorable advocates for us and all of Klal Yisrael.

In accordance with the instructions we received from the people of Jerusalem, who advised us that it was the custom of the Holy City not to visit graves close to Shabbos, we were unable to visit the graves of other holy people buried on Har Hazeisim, for it was already after midday on Friday afternoon. We were also very tired from the exertion; the Rebbe, in particular, had found it very difficult to climb up and down the mountains. It takes at least a full day — possibly more — to cover the entire Har Hazeisim, leaving time to daven at each tzaddik's grave.

We intended to travel to Har Hazeisim again on a different day and visit the graves of tzaddikim such as the Mordechai, Rabbeinu Klonimus, the Bartenura, and others, but in the end we did not have time for this.

The Rebbe inquired about the whereabouts of the burial place of Rabbi Gershon Kitover (the brother-in-law of the Baal Shem Tov) and other holy people buried on Har Hazeisim (such as Rabbi Moshe Galanti), but he was told that the location of those graves is unknown.

The Rebbe was distraught over the fact that in the Holy Land people were unable to care for the graves of tzaddikim of this caliber and ensure that their burial places were marked. He consoled himself by saying that perhaps it was the will of these tzaddikim to have their burial places shrouded in mystery. (This was in keeping with the Arizal's teaching that the grave of a tzaddik reflects on the source of his soul; accordingly, the souls of tzaddikim who have a marked gravesite are rooted in the revealed world, and the souls of those whose gravesites are not marked are rooted in the hidden world.)

On our way down Har Hazeisim, we saw Yad Avshalom, the monument that Avshalom built for himself (as recorded in *II Shmuel* 18:18). We also saw the "House of Freedom" that King Uziyahu built for himself when he became afflicted with *tzaraas* (*II Melachim* 15:5), and the Ben Hinnom valley, about which it is said that Gehinnom will open up there in the future (see *Eruvin* 19a).

DISCUSSIONS WITH THE SABA KADISHA

We left Har Hazeisim and went directly to the home of the Saba Kadisha. He greeted the Rebbe with a joyous countenance and sat the Rebbe beside him as he had done the previous day.

The Rebbe told the Saba Kadisha that he was coming straight from visiting the graves of tzaddikim, and the Saba Kadisha replied, *"Lo ye'uneh latzaddik kol aven* — there will not befall a righteous man any iniquity" (*Mishlei* 12:21).

The Rebbe explained that the Saba Kadisha was referring to the mystical idea that a person requires special protection and deliverance when returning from a cemetery, and the Saba Kadisha answered, "Yes, yes."

The Rebbe and the Saba Kadisha then discussed the question of whether Kohanim are allowed to visit Kever Rachel and other graves of tzaddikim. In the course of this discussion, the Saba Kadisha displayed his mastery over all subjects of the Torah, making reference to the Rebbe's work *Minchas Eluzar* (3:64), in which the issue of Kohanim visiting graves of tzaddikim is discussed. We were amazed by how well-versed the Saba Kadisha was in the writings of our Rebbe, and how he did not forget anything.

Afterward, the Rebbe posed a question to the Saba Kadisha. "When I came to Eretz Yisrael, it was with the intention that I would not do anything without the guidance of our master. I am therefore asking you on which day I should travel to Chevron, where the holy Patriarchs and Matriarchs are buried. I would like to go on Sunday; does our master consent? Or perhaps the roads are still considered dangerous since the massacres of last year; as the Maharil wrote, in times of danger one should not visit the graves of holy ones. Perhaps [his honor] will instruct me not to go to Chevron now at all, in which case I will follow his advice faithfully."

"Why is his honor asking specifically about going on Sunday?" the Saba Kadisha queried.

"Because we do not have much time here in the Holy Land, and we need to plan our itinerary now day by day," the Rebbe replied.

"But why doesn't his honor ask about a different day that week that is better?" the Saba Kadisha continued.

"Perhaps his honor is referring to the Arizal's instruction to Rabbi Chaim Vital not to go to a grave except on the day before Rosh Chodesh or from the 15th of the month and onward?" the Rebbe asked. (The Sunday he had originally asked about was only the 13th of the Hebrew month.)

"There is still time to resolve this question," the Saba Kadisha said. (See The Fifth Day for what we write there.)

The discussion moved to *pilpul* and Aggadah, and the Rebbe derived immense pleasure from this. Afterward, he stood up to receive a parting blessing from the Saba Kadisha, and said that because of the holiness of imminent *Shabbos Kodesh* (it was already about three hours after midday) he would not bother him now, and he asked permission to come again the following day, on Shabbos.

"What time would his honor like to come?" the Saba Kadisha asked.

"About an hour after midday," the Rebbe responded.

To this, the Saba Kadisha answered that he should specify the time according to Eretz Yisrael time, not according to European time, so the Rebbe said that he would come at 7 o'clock Eretz Yisrael time, and the Saba Kadisha indicated his agreement.

CHAPTER 5

THE THIRD DAY

W hen we returned from the home of the Saba Kadisha to the neighborhood where we were staying, we did not even have a chance to rest a bit from our tiring excursions, for we had to begin preparing for the imminent arrival of Shabbos. It was not long before we heard the sound of trumpets and shofars telling the people to stop their work.

We looked around, and the sight that met our eyes was completely novel to us. People were dressed in festive white silk Shabbos clothing to greet the holy Shabbos Queen. Even youths from the age of 13 were wearing white silk clothing and a *shtreimel* on their heads; spiritual beauty, fear of G-d, and chassidus radiated from them. It was among these people that we had the privilege to spend Shabbos. (Unfortunately, there are those who dress themselves in the white silk clothing of the *perushim*, but are really sinners. However, the people with whom we spent Shabbos were truly permeated with the holiness of Torah and chassidus.)

The Rebbe entered the large hall attached to the Tiferes Tzvi shul on the property of Kollel Munkacs that had been prepared in honor of him and his entourage. After Kabbalas Shabbos, the song *Bar Yochai* was sung to a beautiful tune. (The custom in Jerusalem and other cities in Eretz Yisrael is to sing *Bar Yochai* on the Shabbos before Lag BaOmer. In Tzefas, it is sung every Friday night.)

While the song was being sung, the Rebbe was imbued with a fervor of holiness, and began dancing with joy as he said the holy words. The people also sang and danced joyously, in a scene that cannot be described on paper to those who did not witness it.

When the Rebbe arrived at the Friday night *seudah* to sing *Shalom Aleichem*, the hall was packed with people. Despite the crowding, we were delighted to spend Shabbos in Jerusalem in the company of beloved friends, great scholars, *roshei yeshivos*, and their students.

During the *divrei Torah*, the Rebbe spoke in a fiery voice about the war against the Amalek in every generation. He emphasized that in Eretz Yisrael there is an even stronger obligation for every individual to fight against the new factions who departed from the ways of our forefathers, against the Hebrew schools of the Zionists, and

The holy Rebbe surrounded by chassidim

against the flawed ideology of the settlers and farmers who were defiling the Holy Land.

Everyone present trembled at the Rebbe's words. After *Bircas HaMazon*, we danced while singing "*Ranenu tzaddikim* — Sing joyfully, O righteous" (*Tehillim* 33:1), and then everyone went to their homes, happy.

Shabbos morning, the Rebbe davened for the *amud* as was customary, and during the Torah reading all the members of our party had *aliyos* to recite the *Gomel* blessing for having safely crossed the sea. (The Rebbe had already *bentched gomel* on Thursday.)

The Kohanim recited the Priestly Blessing during Shacharis and Mussaf, as is the custom in Jerusalem, and the Rebbe was pleased to hear the blessings (as he was throughout his stay in Eretz Yisrael, where the Priestly Blessing is recited every day).

After Kiddush, it was time for the Rebbe to visit the Saba Kadisha. We began walking through the streets of Jerusalem, carrying with us a bottle of fine aged wine from Eretz Yisrael, as per the Rebbe's request. As we walked, a large crowd gathered behind us. This was despite the Rebbe's repeated pleading that people should not follow him, for he did not wish to cause the Saba Kadisha distress because of crowding.

We arrived at the house of the Saba Kadisha, who looked like an angel, his countenance lustrous. He wished us a good and blessed Shabbos, and the Rebbe gave him the bottle of wine.

"I have brought *bikkurim* to our teacher, the Saba Kadisha,"[1] the Rebbe said. The Saba Kadisha answered that wine is usually detrimental to his health, but if the Rebbe brought it to him it cannot cause him any harm. He made a blessing in a loud sweet voice, drank the wine, and gave a cup to the Rebbe. The two of them drank each other's *shirayim* and made a *l'chaim*.

The Saba Kadisha instructed that wine and the fruits of Eretz Yisrael be served to all those present in honor of the Rebbe. Then they exchanged *divrei Torah* related to wine.

---

1. This was a reference to the Gemara in *Kesubos* 105b, which states that one who brings a gift to a Torah scholar, it is as if he brought *bikkurim*. The Gemara also states (*Yoma* 71a) that if someone wishes to offer wine on the Altar, he should fill the throats of Torah scholars with wine.

On our way home, we saw a large vehicle full of people. It did not occur to me that these were Jews; who would think that Jews could be driving on Shabbos in the Holy City?

But the *chareidi* Jews who were with us indicated that these were indeed people who called themselves Jews, secular Zionists who were not embarrassed to travel by car from Tel Aviv to desecrate Shabbos publicly, even in the courtyards of Hashem in Jerusalem! This scene embittered our hearts.

When we returned, it was several hours after midday, and after resting a bit from walking to and from the Saba Kadisha's house in the heat of the day, we had to quickly eat the Shabbos *seudah*, again with many people in attendance. The Rebbe himself sat at a small table, and everyone stood crowded around him like a wall, but as the Mishnah teaches about the miracles of the Beis HaMikdash, no one ever said it was too crowded for him in Yerushalayim (*Avos* 5:7).

When it was time for *seudah shelishis*, the entire courtyard of the Kollel filled up from end to end, so much so that it was impossible for the Rebbe to walk from the house where he was staying to the hall. It was no longer daytime, and because the *bein hashmashos* (twilight) period in Jerusalem is very short, we did not have time to make place for the Rebbe to pass. We therefore had to stay in the house where we were for *seudah shelishis*. We were joined only by the prominent rabbanim and by the first twenty to thirty other people who managed to enter and merited joining the Rebbe for *seudah shelishis*. Throngs of people surrounded the house, standing at the door and at the windows to hear the *zemiros*.

When it was time to say *divrei Torah*, the Rebbe raised his voice tearfully, bitterly bewailing the exile of the Divine Presence and the Jewish people and G-d's concealed countenance as a result of our sins. He referred to the Yerushalmi that states that if the redemption were to occur between Pesach and Pesach Sheni, all the Jewish people will bring the *pesach*-offering on Pesach Sheni.

"We are now entering the week of Pesach Sheni," the Rebbe said, "and also the week of Lag BaOmer, the yahrtzeit of Rabbi Shimon bar Yochai, who loudly bemoaned the prolonged exile. We daven and hope that Rabbi Shimon bar Yochai should arise to intercede on

Klal Yisrael's behalf to hasten our redemption, and that we should merit to bring the *pesach*-offering this Pesach Sheni in the rebuilt Beis HaMikdash in Jerusalem."

These words, said during *seudah shelishis*, at a time of intense Heavenly favor, aroused a great belief in the coming of Mashiach, and the sound of crying was heard inside and outside. May Hashem put these tears in His flask and may His mercy prevail for the sake of the Jewish people.

CHAPTER 6

THE FOURTH DAY

THE ELDER OF THE KABBALISTS

On Sunday, after Shacharis, the Rebbe traveled to the home of the great, holy Kabbalist, the Kohen Rabbi Chaim Shaul Dweck, who lived in the Bukharan neighborhood. Rabbi Dweck was greatly moved by the Rebbe's sanctity, and they kissed each other's hands with intense emotion.

"Why did you come without notifying us prior to your arrival, so that we could have prepared to greet His Honor?" Rabbi Dweck asked.

The Rebbe answered, "Why is it necessary to make great preparations for us?"

Although Rabbi Dweck had become blind in his old age, his face was saintly. He and the Rebbe sat down together, he sitting cross-legged, as the Sephardim are accustomed to do, and displaying signs of honor and subordination to the Rebbe.

The Rebbe in Torah discussion with Rav Chaim Shaul Dweck

Rabbi Dweck sent immediately to inform his offspring, and the other students of Yeshivah Rechovos HaNahar, of the Rebbe's arrival, and they came to his house with great ceremony. (The Rebbe intended to visit Rabbi Dweck's yeshivah when the rabbi was learning the hidden wisdom of the Torah with the Kabbalists. This did not happen, however, because we were busy with so many other things every day of our stay.)

Rabbi Dweck honored the Rebbe with a priestly gift: his holy writings. In return, the Rebbe promised to send his own writings when he returned home. The Kohen asked that drinks and delicacies be served in honor of his guest, and we were also privileged to partake in this meal in the company of the Torah scholars and tzaddikim.

When the Rebbe parted from Rabbi Dweck, he asked the rabbi to confer upon him the Priestly Blessing. Rabbi Dweck complied, and he then asked the Rebbe to leave a blessing for his household, as well. The Rebbe blessed him and his family, for his wife, the elderly *tzaddekes*, had also come to request the tzaddik's blessing, and he blessed Rabbi Dweck's offspring, as well.

Rabbi Dweck and all who were with him escorted the Rebbe to his automobile. The Rebbe asked him not to exert himself too much, and they parted.[1]

After that, we visited the home of the great Rabbi Yitzchak Frankel, the noted *dayan* of the Ashkenazi community in Jerusalem, and one of the leaders and most important members of Kollel Munkacs and the Ten Suburbs.

ETERNAL CHESSED

As we were traveling, we noticed a funeral procession. When the Rebbe saw the procession from a distance, he descended from the automobile to fulfill the mitzvah of accompanying the dead at least four cubits. When he inquired who the deceased was, he was told that it was a woman, the granddaughter of the holy Rabbi Aharon HaLevi of Strasheleh, a student of the Baal HaTanya and the author of the *Avodas HaLevi* and other holy works. When the Rebbe heard this, he was seized with trepidation, and he said, "The granddaugh-

---

1. It is told that several days before Rabbi Dweck's passing, the poverty in his house reached critical proportions, to the point that his attendants approached him to ask what they should eat on Shabbos, for there was no money for Shabbos expenses. Rabbi Dweck answered, "*Ein od milvado*," there is no power other than Hashem.

Some time before that, in the city Munkacs, the Rebbe gave his attendants a *kvittel* (a note requesting his prayer and blessing) with 500 crowns to send to Rabbi Dweck. It arrived in Jerusalem that Friday. When the joyful news was conveyed to Rabbi Dweck, he answered, "Didn't I tell you that there is no power other than Hashem?" Then he blessed the Rebbe profusely, concluding, "The main thing is that his flame should never be extinguished."

That evening, when the Rebbe lit Chanukah lights, the eighth light kept going out. The Rebbe relit it several times, but it took a number of attempts until it remained lit. Later, when the Rebbe came to the Friday night *seudah*, he saw that the flame that had been lit with the candle inherited from the Bnei Yissas'char had gone out by itself. The Rebbe said to his attendant, Rabbi Chaim Ber, "Who knows what the holy Rabbi Chaim Shaul Dweck is doing in Jerusalem?" Indeed, on the following Monday, Rabbi Dweck passed away.

ter of the holy Rabbi Aharon! Hashem made it happen that I should escort this daughter of holy ones in the land of the living."

The Rebbe accompanied the bier until the end of the street. All those who saw him joined the funeral procession as well, and this resulted in great honor for the deceased and her ancestors.

On that day, it was no longer possible for us to go anywhere, since we were exhausted from the exertion of the previous day (Shabbos). In the afternoon, we busied ourselves with the needs of the community, calling a meeting for the people of our Kollel, as will be described later, and arranging urgent matters related to the Kollel and its members.

Divine Secrets to the G–d–Fearing

That night was Pesach Sheni, and after Maariv it was once again time to visit the Saba Kadisha. When we arrived at his home he was lying in bed, still suffering from the illness that had led to his recent hospitalization. His face was happy, and he was smoking a cigarette. He honored the Rebbe with a cigarette as well. The Rebbe asked that no one should remain with them in the house, for he wanted to speak to the Saba Kadisha privately.

From outside, we were able to overhear parts of the conversation. We realized that they were discussing the ultimate redemption, and we trembled.

The Rebbe read to the Saba Kadisha a letter that had been written to him by his father-in-law, the holy Rabbi Yaakov Moshe of Kamarna. It was written in Yiddish script, but the Saba Kadisha was able to read only the traditional Hebrew print used in holy writings. Part of the letter read:

"I saw your holy father today in a dream [he had passed away that year] and I said to him tearfully, 'My dear *mechutan*, why is this exile so prolonged?' He answered me, 'Believe me, in the upper world there is a great deal of distress over this, but they are waiting for the earthly tzaddik who has the power to decree…'"

"You are the tzaddik of the generation," the Rebbe told the Saba Kadisha. He begged him to decree that Mashiach should reveal himself speedily, in honor of the Divine Presence and for the benefit of the Jewish people, for the exile was no longer bearable." How much longer can the *churban* of the world continue?" the Rebbe pleaded.

The Saba Kadisha answered in his great humility, "I am not a tzaddik."

The Rebbe persisted, however, and the two spoke about this subject for a long time. We could not hear how they resolved the matter, and we cannot write much about it. The Rebbe himself did not reveal to anyone the details of the discussion. (On the following Rosh Hashanah, when the Rebbe spoke before the blowing of the shofar, to arouse

The Kamarna Rebbe, Rav Yaakov Moshe Safrin, father-in-law of the Rebbe

people to *teshuvah* and to invoke Heavenly mercy, he said publicly that when he had asked the Saba Kadisha about the time of the redemption, the Saba had replied that it was imminent.)

The Rebbe also discussed with the Saba Kadisha other lofty matters and issues related to himself and his family. The Saba Kadisha asked the Rebbe which of the acknowledged leaders of the generation he considered to be trustworthy. After he heard the Rebbe's answer, he expressed his own opinion.

They continued exchanging stories and talking for two hours — a very long time.

KOLLEL MUNKACS AND THE TEN SUBURBS

Jewish settlement in Eretz Yisrael is comprised of Jews from cities all over the world who left their homelands at great personal sacrifice to devote themselves to Torah and service of G-d in the Holy Land. The Jews of the Diaspora traditionally contributed tzedakah via the Kollelim and Rabbi Meir Baal Haness funds to support these righteous individuals. This system of financial support was established

The Rebbe with Rav Moshe Goldstein,
author of "Mass'os Yerushalayim"

by the great luminaries of previous generations — such as the Ramban, Beis Yosef, Alshich, Arizal, and others — and was continued by the leaders of the Jewish people in every generation.

It was beautiful for us to see Torah scholars and righteous people in Eretz Yisrael desisting from all mundane pursuits, their primary occupation being service of G-d, day and night. Some of these people devoted themselves exclusively to Gemara and halachah — the revealed portions of Torah — while some devoted themselves to the secrets of the Torah. Others spent their time davening and saying Tehillim, while others involved themselves with good deeds and opposing those who were tearing down Torah observance. There are also those who involved themselves in all of these things. Our Kollel boasted people from all these categories. What these people had in common was a spirit of holiness and purity, devotion to the service of Hashem.

Among these holy Kollelim, Kollel Munkacs and the Ten Suburbs was exceptional for its spiritual standing. The Kollel was directed by the Rebbe, and one of his many reasons for traveling to Eretz Yisrael was to observe the quality of the Kollel members.

That night, the night of Pesach Sheni, all the members of Kollel Munkacs gathered in the Tiferes Tzvi shul to discuss a number of urgent matters related to the Kollel. As the Kollel's administrator and secretary, I was present at the meeting.

The Rebbe spoke about the situation of the Kollel in Eretz Yisrael and the Diaspora, and described how the burdens of the exile and of earning a livelihood had become increasingly difficult for the Jews of the Diaspora. Nevertheless, he said, the Jews of the Diaspora do not forget the love of Jerusalem, and they practically take bread out of their mouths to support their brethren in Eretz Yisrael.

The Rebbe also said that he sees now with his own eyes how the members of the Kollel conduct themselves, and he is convinced that they are exceptional, especially the great Torah scholars among them. But because of the terrible situation prevailing in the Holy Land, there is a need for increased vigilance in adhering to the statutes of the Kollel that were instituted as a safeguard of the holy Torah already during the times of the Rebbe's father and the other tzaddikim who founded the Kollel. No breach should be made in these statutes; each man should stand guard over the members of his household to ensure that their clothing is modest, and should protect his sons and daughters and grandchildren from becoming ensnared in the satanic Hebrew schools that have claimed many victims. Although it is unnecessary to warn the members of our Kollel against these things, who knows what will happen in the future as the forces of impurity gain momentum.

The members of the Kollel accepted once again for themselves and their children to adhere to the following statutes:

1. To follow the traditions of our forefathers and early rabbis, both in matters related to prayer and in matters related to learning, without any change, Heaven forbid.

2. To ensure that prayer with a *minyan* should never be missed — morning and evening, every day, during the week as well as on Shabbos and Yom Tov.

3. To establish at least one set time every day that ten men learn Torah together in the beis medrash.

4. To see to it that the Mishnayos *shiurim* in the merit of the departed donors to the Kollel's endowment fund should take place only in this beis medrash, at all times, according to the statutes.

5. All members of the Kollel (even those living far away in the Old City) — young and old — are obligated to come at least once during the week to pray one of the daily prayers in this beis medrash and to participate in the aforementioned learning of Mishnayos. In addition, they are obligated to come on Shabbos at least once every two months.

6. To maintain an extreme distance between holy institutions and those who send their sons or daughters to schools that are not conducted in the holy spirit of the traditional *chinuch* passed down from our forefathers.

7. To ensure that the steady congregants in the beis medrash should wear distinctive clothing, should have the image of G-d on their faces (i.e., they should not shave their beards at all, even with scissors, and they should not let their frontal hair grow long), and should conduct themselves in the age-old Jewish spirit.

8. In the women's section, righteous women should make sure that women do not enter wearing immodest clothing, especially not with their hair exposed, even the slightest bit from the side. In addition, a wig that is the same as hair should not be seen or found.

9. To gather in the beis medrash for a public *shalosh seudos* on Shabbos, at the time of Heavenly favor, in keeping with the chassidic tradition passed down to us from our teacher, the holy Baal Shem Tov and his disciples, as is customary throughout the Jewish world.

10. When choosing a *chazzan* or public speaker, the people should select only those who are known to be righteous — i.e., they, their wives, and their sons and daughters conduct themselves in the way that is proper for Jewish men and women.

11. A person who is not looked upon favorably by the genuine *chareidim* in the Holy City should not deliver a lecture in the beis medrash, whether on Torah topics or on any other topics.

12. Every individual has a holy obligation to be vigilant regarding these statutes and not violate them at all, but rather to keep them himself and see to it that his children should keep them eternally. These statutes will be a sign and a protection for the holy Torah law, and he who follows them should be blessed.

I hereby approve and uphold these statutes with the help of Hashem.

He who awaits the speedy salvation of Hashem and the complete redemption, for the sake of His Name with love.

Chaim Eluzar Shapira
Director of Kollel Munkacs and the Ten Suburbs
in the Holy Land

Another issue that was raised was that the members of our Kollel lived in the Old City, while the property of our Kollel was in the new city. As a result, our members are spread over various batei medrash and yeshivos most of the day, to learn Torah and serve Hashem.

In keeping with the statutes, the members of the Kollel would gather once or twice a day for a regular Mishnayos *shiur* in the merit of the departed donors to the endowment fund of our Kollel. The Rebbe derived great pleasure from seeing the members, scholars and G-d-fearing individuals, gathering in the beis medrash, learning Mishnayos together morning and evening, lighting olive oil, and davening and saying Kaddish for the sake of the departed souls. He said that he is confident that they will accomplish much good in the upper spheres for those souls by virtue of their learning in Jerusalem in their merit. Nevertheless, it would be a significant improvement if the members of the Kollel would conduct their

Torah *shiurim* and their entire daily service of Hashem in the beis medrash of our Kollel, with all of them present.

During this discussion, the question of whether a yeshivah could be established in the Tiferes Tzvi beis medrash arose. The other Kollelim in the Holy Land housed yeshivos in their facilities where people old and young could learn. The duty of those in the yeshivah was to increase the honor of the Torah, and they would receive increased stipends from the Kollel.

At that gathering, the Yeshivah Tiferes Tzvi was established in the beis medrash.

In view of the urgent need for housing, we also decided to begin construction of a second building on the Kollel's property, which would contain four spacious apartments for Kollel families (who would be selected by drawing of lots, as was customary). This construction would be financed by money donated by generous Jews to rebuild the ruins of Jerusalem, which is a great mitzvah whose fruits are enjoyed in this world and whose principal remains for the next world. (Now, *baruch Hashem*, they are about to complete this building, and one mitzvah follows another — because so many people donated to our Kollel's fund, a third building is about to be built.)

Several other matters related to the operation of the Kollel were decided then, and the discussions lasted until after midnight.

CHAPTER 7

THE FIFTH DAY

KING AND KOHEN

On Monday morning, Pesach Sheni, the great Kohen and tzaddik, Rabbi Chaim Shaul Dweck, arrived at the Rebbe's lodgings. He was accompanied by his son and other scholars of Yeshivah Rechovos HaNahar. The Rebbe rejoiced at his arrival, showing him much honor, and the two delighted in mutual love.

Rabbi Dweck asked the Rebbe to encourage the scholars in his holy yeshivah, both verbally and in writing, and the Rebbe promised to write a strong letter from his house urging donors to support the students of Kabbalah in this yeshivah. (Of course, the Rebbe kept his promise when he returned to Munkacs.)

The Rebbe also asked the Kohen to give him a blessing, which he did. (Those of us standing around also merited that the Kohen rested his hands on us and gave us the Priestly Blessing.) May G-d in His mercy consent to his blessing, and bless us all among the remainder of the Jewish people.

THE TOMBS OF THE DAVIDIC KINGS

On that day, we obtained the necessary permit to enter Mount Zion and the tombs of the Davidic kings. The police officials opened the gate of Mount Zion, where the kings of the Davidic dynasty are buried in a cave. Above the tombs are beautiful buildings.

When we arrived there, the Rebbe prepared himself, with trepidation, to enter. His emotion extended to us, causing us to focus at least slightly on the place we were entering: the burial place of David HaMelech, his son Shlomo, and the other great kings of the Davidic dynasty.

When we approached the entrance to the outer room, the Arab and British officers warned us not to say Tehillim at the tomb inside, for it was forbidden by the law and the government. When the Rebbe heard this, he was seized with fear, and his face paled.

These words were like sharp swords piercing our hearts. We were infuriated, for we had not known beforehand about this evil law. How could they dare act as though they owned the praises of David HaMelech and forbid them from being recited at his holy resting place? But that was the situation, and we saw fulfilled before our own eyes the lament of David HaMelech (*Tehillim* 89:51-52): "Remember, O L-rd, the taunt of Your servant...that Your enemies have taunted, O Hashem, that they have taunted the footsteps of Your Messiah."

They brought us from the outer room to the inner room, and they instructed us to leave our shoes behind and enter barefoot. We reached an iron barrier blocking the way to a third room, where it is said that the coffin of one of their sheiks lay. We saw a long, golden cover spread over the coffin of his impure corpse, and they would not let anyone go past the barrier. The Rebbe stood opposite the entrance leading to the innermost room, and began reciting Tehillim quietly, by heart. "A psalm of Asaph: O G-d! The nations have entered into Your inheritance, they have defiled the sanctuary..." he murmured brokenheartedly. He cried, but his voice was barely heard.

Kever of David HaMelech on Mount Zion

The evil officer warned us repeatedly not to raise our voices. Our lips moved, but our voices were not heard. After about ten minutes, the officer said that it was enough, and we had to leave.

We consoled ourselves with the knowledge that at least we had merited to be in close proximity to royalty and to stand near the holy resting place of the Davidic kings. May Hashem remember the covenant of David, the anointed king, may the Mashiach arrive speedily and gladden our hearts, and may others no longer inherit his honor.

The Rebbe was deeply distressed that the holiness and honor of the kings was so desecrated, to the point where he almost regretted visiting the ruins of Mount Zion, a place of such sanctity. The reason for his regret was that one does not go to see a king in his disgrace, and woe to the eyes that see this.

He also said that now he understands what the Saba Kadisha meant with his answer to the question of whether to visit the graves of the Patriarchs in Chevron. The Saba Kadisha had answered that there was still time to decide this. Now, the Rebbe said that he himself has decided not to travel there, for the holy Me'aras HaMachpelah was also controlled by these wild nations, and there, as well, it is forbidden to enter; one could only stand at a distance, near the wall. How could we see this disgrace of our holy forefathers?

After that we went to visit the large shul that is traced back to the Tanna, Rabbi Yochanan ben Zakkai. This awe-inspiring shul is a beautiful building in the Old City.

We also went to the beis medrash of the holy Kabbalist, Rabbi Sar Shalom Sharabi. By then, it was after midday. In the shul, we found Sephardic Jews (and among them a hidden Ashkenazi tzaddik) sitting on low benches and studying the hidden wisdom of the Torah from the Arizal's *Pri Eitz Chaim*, which one person was reading aloud before them.

The Rebbe sat with them for about a quarter of an hour to learn with them. They were so awed by him, it was as though they were mute in his presence. They wished to honor him to read before them so that they could learn from him, but he declined, telling them not to interrupt their learning. So they learned as they were accustomed to, with the Rebbe among them. He approved greatly of their collec-

The Yochanan ben Zakkai Shul in the Old City of Jerusalem

tive study of Kabbalah, which they learned in awe and in fear, and then he left.

On that day, Monday, the Rebbe did not visit the Saba Kadisha. The reason he gave was that he wished to fulfill the precept (*Vayikra* 16:2), "He shall not come at all times to the sanctuary."

We ate the Pesach Sheni meal in the company of beloved friends, prominent rabbanim, tzaddikim, chassidim and zealots — who stand guard in the Holy City against the secular destroyers of the religion.

The Rebbe drew this holy group of zealots close, and showed them love. They, in turn, turned their ears to him to seek G-d's word, so that he could enlighten them in the path of the authentic tradition of the Jewish spirit.

CHAPTER 8

THE SIXTH DAY

Tuesday morning, one of the outstanding scholars of Jerusalem honored the Rebbe to be both *sandek* and *mohel* at his son's *bris*, and everyone saw the Rebbe's skill in performing this holy mitzvah. This was the first time he had merited to perform a *bris milah* in the Holy City of Jerusalem (see more on this in The Seventh Day), and he stayed for the *seudah* afterwards.

On this day we were very busy seeing to the affairs of our Kollel Tiferes Tzvi. Following the counsel of Shlomo HaMelech (*Mishlei* 11:14), that "salvation lies with much counsel," we met with the members of the Kollel's committee who live in Eretz Yisrael to discuss and resolve matters of concern. We also traversed the property of the Kollel in order to choose the best place to build suitable housing.

In addition, we listened to the cries of the needy members of our Kollel who were pleading for money from our fund. They begged us to improve their situation, for their needs were numerous. Nevertheless, despite their poverty they dedicated their lives to Torah and fear of G-d. If only the office of our Kollel could provide relief to all of the needy in Eretz Yisrael! If our benefactors in the Diaspora would visit Eretz Yisrael and observe their beloved brothers there, their hearts would burn to help them and support them generously.

The leaders and administrators of other Rabbi Meir Baal Haness Kollelim, as well as yeshivos and charitable institutions in Jerusalem also pleaded with the Rebbe to honor them with a visit to their institutions. Although he held many of the Kollelim in Eretz Yisrael in high esteem, there was not enough time to visit them all. Besides, he did not want to single out one over the other, so he could not make exceptions. He therefore visited only our own Kollel, despite his busy schedule, since it was under the mantle of his leadership. To his flock, he was a faithful shepherd, lovingly pursuing their well-being.

The Rebbe's son-in-law was due to arrive on this day by ship at the port of Jaffa. He was supposed to arrive in Jerusalem in the morning, but he was delayed by the overzealous border inspectors, due to visa issues. When I returned around midday from Har Hazeisim (where I had gone with my relatives to visit the grave of my grandfather, the chassid Moshe Aharon Reichman, *Av Beis Din* of Novisonitz), I saw that the Rebbe was greatly distressed over the delay. I sent a special messenger to Jaffa, and after some intervention, the Rebbe's son-in-law finally arrived at his destination toward evening. The Rebbe greeted him joyously, and we were relieved.

After Maariv, the Rebbe went with his son-in-law, Rav Baruch, to the holy abode of the Saba Kadisha, who was lying on his bed, his face glowing with holiness. When the Rebbe introduced his son-in-law, the Saba Kadisha greeted him warmly and said, "May G-d be gracious to you, my son, blessed is He and blessed is His Name, and may He indeed be blessed." (This was a play on words, for his name was Baruch.) The Saba Kadisha continued to shower him with blessings that made reference to verses related to his other names, Yehoshua Yerachmiel, and the Rebbe was delighted.

The Saba Kadisha then asked Rav Baruch about several other matters.

After that, the Saba Kadisha continued speaking to the Rebbe, characteristically carrying the discussion from one topic to another, including *divrei Torah*. I believe it was at this time that we heard the Saba Kadisha tell the Rebbe that in the year 5600 (1840), at the time of the famous blood libel against the Jews of Damascus, he was one of those who fought valiantly against the evil libelers. (The miracle that happened afterwards to save the Jews was by virtue of the intervention of Sir Moses Montefiore.) The Saba Kadisha also mentioned that the great Rabbi Yaakov Elfandri, author of *Mutzal MeiEish*, was his father's grandfather.

CHAPTER 9

THE SEVENTH DAY

On Wednesday, we awoke early. This was a holy day for us, the day when we would merit visiting Kever Rachel and pouring our hearts out there.

At about 8 a.m. (European time, the equivalent of 2 p.m. Eretz Yisrael time), we traveled to Kever Rachel in Bethlehem. When we were able to see the holy site, we experienced indescribable excitement and awe. Although we were fearful of entering, the yearning and love we felt propelled us to enter the inner sanctuary. It was already full of men (and women at the side) who had arrived before us to hear the Rebbe praying in the resting place of the holy Matriarch.

We put on tefillin in preparation for Shacharis, and we were seized with awe when we watched the Rebbe standing and pouring his heart out in prayer. If only we could merit to pray like that on Rosh Hashanah and Yom Kippur, we would be happy.

After he had finished davening and removing his tefillin, the Rebbe stood before Hashem wrapped in his tallis. He approached the holy tomb with humility and trepidation, holding the siddur of the Arizal, and began reciting verses of supplication from the *Tikkun*

A view of the building housing Kever Rachel

Chatzos of Rachel. As recited the verse (*Yirmiyah* 31:14), "A voice is heard on high, wailing, bitter weeping, Rachel weeps for her children," his every limb heaved and trembled as he cried and recited supplications.

The Rebbe raised his voice in holiness and said:

> Rachel, our Holy Mother, awaken! Awaken for
> the sake of your children and please go to your
> holy husband and the other holy Patriachs and
> Matriarchs to awaken them — [for] we cannot even
> go to Me'aras HaMachpelah to pray — and cry out
> and pray together to redeem the Jewish people and
> the holy Divine Presence from bondage. Look at the
> condition of your children, who are spread out and
> scattered among the nations, in all the countries,
> oppressed and dejected. Woe! Know that there are
> two million Jews in Soviet Russia experiencing total
> religious persecution to tear them away from our
> faith, and there is no one to rescue them. In our
> Holy Land, see how they have butchered without
> pity, and killed holy ones of your children; no one
> was gracious or merciful. Torah scholars [in the

Kever Rachel

Holy Land] are afflicted and learn Torah amid pressure and poverty; and in other countries, [see] what the officers and rulers have done — they afflict [your children] and are exceedingly evil, they have restricted the livelihood of the Jews. Children ask for bread and there is none, and there is no money to pay for the costs of teaching Torah to the children. All of the time limits of the exile have passed and there is no longer strength to endure the physical and spiritual suffering, for each day is worse than the one before, as the forces of heresy gain strength from all sides — it is literally a generation of *shmad*.

And you — our Patriarchs and Matriarchs, arise and intervene on our behalf, for the trials are beyond our capacity and the concealment of G-d's countenance is infinite. Now is no longer the time to be still; until when will you sleep restfully? Until when, our Holy Mother, will you not exercise your power to ask, "Where is the promise of 'And the children will return to their border'?" Didn't Hashem, in His Honor, promise you that there is reward for your accomplishment? Therefore, you should not be quiet and you should not refrain from crying out until Hashem tells Zion, "Arise," and the pride of the Jewish people and of the Torah is raised and His Sanctuary is rebuilt speedily.

The spiritual awakening at the time was extraordinary, and copious tears were shed by all in attendance.

It is difficult to believe that we merited walking along the path where Rachel's holy husband Yaakov had walked when he buried her, the place where he laid her tombstone. The tombstone remains there until today (although it is impossible to see because it is surrounded by a high building constructed many years ago to spare it from being touched and ruined by outsiders).

The Rebbe bemoaned the fact that not even a small opening was left through which one could peek to see the holy stone that Yaakov Avinu himself had laid. But since the wall was already built and closed up, who would not be afraid to touch a corner of it? The words uttered by the Rebbe's holy mouth were like sparks of fire; they made us tremble and were inscribed on our hearts forever.

After that we recited Tehillim together intently and said the *Yehi Ratzon* supplication begging Hashem to be receptive to our prayers. Then the Rebbe read the *kvitlach* that he had brought with him from outside Eretz Yisrael and the requests from those in Eretz Yisrael, and these *kvitlach* were left at the resting place of our Holy Mother.

The Rebbe said that even though the *kvitlach* contained personal requests, Rachel would certainly not be upset. A mother's mercy on her children is boundless, he said, and Rachel would undoubtedly have mercy on us and bring our prayers — general and specific — to the Throne of Glory, so that they could come to fruition. She would also surely place our rivers of tears into the heavenly jug to open the gates of salvation.

After all the prayers and supplications had been completed, beverages and pastries brought from Jerusalem were distributed. The

Rebbe drank and made a *l'chaim*, and with his cheeks still wet from the tears he had shed, he told of an incident that had taken place with his ancestor, Rabbi Naftali Tzvi of Ropshitz. Once, when the Ropshitzer was intoxicated, he quipped in his holiness, "*L'chaim*, Master of the Universe! May it be Your will that You should merit to have *nachas* from Your children, whom You carried from their birth!"

The Rebbe concluded, "We will say the same to Rachel, our Holy Mother — *l'chaim*, and may she merit to derive much *nachas* from the Jewish people and be a joyful mother of children speedily, in our days." And all those present answered "Amen."

A prominent member of our party, from Jerusalem, said in a lighter vein that when an important guest — a beloved son — comes to visit his mother for a short time, she becomes very excited and joyful and does everything he wants lovingly. Today, he said, a prestigious son came to visit our Holy Mother in her sanctuary, and she certainly derives pleasure and will be filled with mercy upon you, upon us, and upon all of Klal Yisrael.

We went outside, and the Rebbe surveyed the area around this holy place, where Arab corpses are buried. The Rebbe told us that at first, when Sir Moses Montefiore had set out to expand and reinforce the building over Rachel's gravesite, the rabbis of the Diaspora had disapproved. Their objection was based on the Arizal's teaching that the Matriarch Leah belongs to the hidden world, and her resting place is therefore hidden in Me'aras HaMachpelah, while the Matriarch Rachel belongs to the revealed world, and her resting place is therefore open, on the roadside, and not hidden under a building.

But when the rabbis later heard from experts in the Holy Land that impure corpses had been buried around Rachel's tomb, they said that they approved of what Montefiore had done, for the wall would act as a barrier between the holy and the profane, and would be an honor for Rachel. In fact, without this barrier it would not have been possible to pray at her resting place, as the Arizal writes that one should not pray at a grave that is in the vicinity of non-Jewish graves. But now, Rachel's tomb remains undefiled because of the wall surrounding it.

On our way back to Jerusalem, we were shown the place where Binyamin was born and Rachel died.

The entire way back, those who had been with us at Kever Rachel — the chassidim, the God-fearing people, the Torah scholars — could not find the words to describe how the memory of the excitement they had just experienced would remain with them forever. They were simply unable to describe the feelings that would never leave them. Someone said that even though it was customary for the Jews of Eretz Yisrael to pour their hearts out at Kever Rachel with tears and supplications and public *Tikkun Chatzos* — especially during the month of Elul, the days of mercy and forgiveness — they had never experienced such a tremendous spiritual awakening. Now, they said, they had become aware of how holy this awesome place was, and how one should humble himself and completely divest himself of every trace of the mundane before praying at Kever Rachel.

That afternoon, I went with my dear friend, Rav David Shapira, a distinguished member of our Kollel, to the home of the Saba Kadisha. When I arrived, I was horrified to see the Saba Kadisha lying on his sickbed suffering terribly. (It was

Rav David Shapira

said that he had a digestive ailment.) Despite his condition, he inquired as to the well-being of the Rebbe and asked about all of his affairs. He was delighted when Rav David told him about the tremendous spiritual awakening that the Rebbe had brought about at Kever Rachel, and he also enjoyed hearing that on the previous day the Rebbe had acted as both *sandek* and *mohel* with great skill.

The Saba Kadisha inquired about every detail: Did the Rebbe join the *seudah* of the *bris*? Who were the people present there? (From the way the conversation proceeded, I understood that his intention was to inquire about a certain rav from Jerusalem about whom distasteful rumors had circulated with regard to his persecution of the *chareidim* and

The Rebbe in Jerusalem speaking to Rav David Shapira

zealots in the Holy City. Both sides had agreed to ask the Rebbe to adjudicate the dispute. After that, the Saba Kadisha asked me whether the Rebbe was planning to visit him that day, and I answered, "Yes, he plans to come this evening to receive a parting blessing before traveling tomorrow to Tzefas and Meron for Lag BaOmer."

The Saba Kadisha answered, "Tell him not to come today; better he should come tomorrow." I asked him what time, and he said, "Whatever time he wishes." He then said that he wished to daven Minchah. We received a parting blessing from him, and we left.

The door to his room remained open, and I saw how the Saba Kadisha made great efforts to descend from the bed. He donned his outer garment, stood and prayed near his bed, then returned to his bed after reciting Shemoneh Esrei.

Prayer at the Kosel

Toward evening, we went with the Rebbe to the Kosel to daven Minchah before our trip the following day. Aside from the many people who came with the Rebbe to the Kosel, we found that there were many God-fearing and pious individuals there, and also women who had come to pour out their hearts at the holy wall.

The people there were praying, or saying Tehillim, or reciting the holy *Zohar*, and so on. The inhabitants of the Holy Land also prayed at the Kosel for their brethren in the Diaspora and for all those who supported them and their Torah learning, mentioning the donors' names for blessing. There were also members of Kollel Munkacs and the Ten Suburbs who came to the Kosel every day to daven Minchah and Maariv and to pray for those who donate to the Rabbi Meir Baal Haness funds. May Hashem hear their prayers together with all the prayers of the Jewish people.

CHAPTER 10

THE EIGHTH DAY

THE TRIP TO TZEFAS

On Thursday, we prepared to travel by automobile to Meron and Tzefas for Lag BaOmer. In the morning after Shacharis, we stopped at the Ruchamah neighborhood to receive the Saba Kadisha's parting blessing.

When the Rebbe arrived at the Saba Kadisha's house and found him on his sickbed, he was aghast. The Saba Kadisha's face looked different than it had previously, and the Rebbe inquired as to his well-being. At that time it was not yet known that the Saba Kadisha had a lung infection, and we certainly did not dream that his illness was critical. His attendant told us that the Saba had expressed his distress that the yahrtzeit of Rabbi Shimon bar Yochai was approaching, and he was confined to his bed.

The Saba Kadisha asked the Rebbe to sit for a while, but the Rebbe answered that he did not wish to burden the tzaddik at this time with conversation. He added that we had a trip ahead of us.

The Rebbe received the Saba Kadisha's permission to go and a blessing for a successful trip. Then he blessed the Saba Kadisha that he should have a speedy recovery, adding that he hoped to find him completely healthy when we returned to Jerusalem.

We set out on our journey with heavy hearts, distraught that we were leaving the tzaddik in such a state. We were confident, however, that just as he had been critically ill several weeks earlier and with Hashem's help had recovered, he would soon recover this time, too.

As we made our way past the breathtaking mountains and valleys surrounding Jerusalem, we realized how exceedingly good the land of Eretz Yisrael is. We were also amazed by the tempting fruits and produce growing in the fields and vineyards. The Rebbe was delighted to see this, and he remarked, "How nice and how sweet is the good land that Hashem gave us."

But at the same time, we were disturbed and pained when we passed by the dwellings of Arabs, whose actions are repulsive, and the settlements of non-observant Jews, whose behavior was not in keeping with the holiness of the land. These people did not recognize Hashem and did not keep the Torah, and their conduct distressed us. May they be mercifully purified and spared from punishment.

We also passed between Mount Gerizim and Mount Ebal. Mount Gerizim is now the dwelling place of the Cuthites, who are known as the Samaritans. These people are an independent nation — they have their own so-called "Beis HaMikdash," and they deny the Oral Torah. May Hashem save us and ensure that they never join the Jewish people.

THE CITY OF SHECHEM

We arrived in the city of Shechem, the burial place of Yosef HaTzaddik and his two sons, Menashe and Ephraim. The Rebbe had planned to visit Shechem, the place that had been captured by Yaakov, and daven at Yosef's tomb. To our dismay, however, we did not merit to do so. The Jerusalemites traveling ahead of us

Members of the group visiting Kever Yosef in Shechem

waited for us in Shechem to warn us not to enter, for the following day was a holiday for the Arabs, who had called a strike in protest of the judgment handed down by the government to hang three Arabs who had led the murderers of the Jews the previous year (5689 / 1929). Now, toward evening, we were told, the Arabs are preparing for their protest, and it is not advisable to appear before them during their time of anger — especially in Shechem, the city that is predisposed to misfortune. In addition, there is no Jewish population in Shechem now, and it is therefore better not to enter this dangerous place.

Having no choice, we left Shechem. We hoped to visit Shechem again on Sunday on the way back to Jerusalem, but it did not work out then either. When we came to Shechem toward evening on Sunday, we were warned again that it was inopportune to visit the holy tomb so late in the day. However, the members of our group who arrived in Shechem prior to sundown did visit the grave of Yosef.

The Rebbe later noted that he had not managed to visit the graves of any of the seven shepherds, the holy *Ushpizin* (Avraham, Yitzchak, Yaakov, Moshe, Aharon, Yosef and David). Although he had visited the tombs of the Davidic kings on Mount Zion, he had been allowed to enter only the outer chambers, and he had come away from there deeply troubled. He had merited visiting only the grave of the Matriarch Rachel — may she arise in our defense, and arouse all of the seven shepherds and all of the tzaddikim to fulfill our wishes for good.

We passed the holy city of Teveriah and Lake Kinneret, and in the evening we reached Tzefas.

THE NIGHT OF LAG BAOMER

Upon our arrival in Tzefas, we felt new stirrings of holiness. This was the city where great men had dwelled. In the time of the Beis Yosef and the Arizal, Tzefas had boasted an unparalleled generation of Jewish leaders, people who merited Divine inspiration. How fortunate we were to be able to tread upon the ground of this holy city.

The members of the Sanzer beis medrash, founded by the chassidim of the holy Divrei Chaim and his son, the Shiniver Rav, were awaiting us. They had come to ask the Rebbe to join them in their shul for davening — now, and on Shabbos as well. The Rebbe consented, and we proceeded immediately to the beis medrash for Maariv.

After davening, the people in the beis medrash lit a bonfire, as was customary on the night of Lag BaOmer in many cities in Eretz Yisrael.

In preparation for the lighting, they prepared large bowls full of tattered clothing soaked in oil and placed them on a roof near the beis medrash. (Their roofs were flat, not sloped like ours.) We stood inside the fence of the beis medrash, from where the bonfire was lit with a long wooden pole and a torch.

The Rebbe was honored to be the first to ignite the bonfire. When it was lit, the pious people danced and clapped and sang praises to Hashem in the designated special tune, in honor of the Tanna Rabbi Shimon bar Yochai and his son Rabbi Eluzar. They sang *"Va'amarten ko lechai"* and *"Amar Rabbi Akiva, ashreichem Yisrael,"* and afterwards they danced and sang *"Bar Yochai, nimshachta ashrecha"* (Bar Yochai! You were annointed, you are fortunate) in a sweet tune, with the Rebbe among them.

After that a 3-year-old boy was brought to the beis medrash, for the custom was to cut the hair of 3-year-old boys for the first time on Lag BaOmer (just as in Meron, where boys are brought for their first haircut, and the fathers of the boys wear Shabbos clothing and *shtreimels* and dance and praise Hashem). This child was wearing beautiful clothing, and he looked sweet and innocent, with his *peyos* neatly arranged. His hair was cut in the beis medrash, cakes and beverages were distributed, and everyone danced joyously. The father held the child on his shoulders, and then his relatives did so as well, dancing with him around and around.

Close to midnight, through the windows of Tzefas, we saw the fire burning at the gravesite of Rabbi Shimon bar Yochai. The joy in Meron during that entire night was boundless. Upon the advice of the *chareidim* in Jerusalem and Tzefas, however, the Rebbe had decided not to travel to Meron at night. Unfortunately, Meron on the night of Lag BaOmer had both good and evil elements, for Zionist boys and girls danced together and behaved frivolously at the holy site, woe to them and to their souls in this world and the next.

On the morning of Lag BaOmer, on our way from Tzefas to Meron, we met them returning from Meron. The males and females were mingling and singing together. Our eyes saw this, and our ears heard, to our great regret. It is most dangerous and invites retribution to behave this way at the tomb of the holy Tanna.

CHAPTER 11

THE NINTH DAY

LAG BAOMER

Friday morning, we set out by automobile to Meron with excitement and trepidation. The entire way, we saw people making their way there is if they were on the way to a joyous celebration, some by car or bus, some on horseback, and some on foot. The path to Meron is narrow, and in one place we had to wait as one automobile left and another one entered.

A festive atmosphere prevailed, especially when we arrived in Meron. From a distance, we could see throngs of people celebrating at the tomb of Rabbi Shimon bar Yochai and his son Rabbi Eluzar. When we came to the large courtyard outside the tomb, men, women, and children were gathered there, filling the courtyard to capacity.

When the Rebbe arrived, people came toward him with dancing and musical instruments in honor of the yahrtzeit. It was very crowded, however, and when the people approached to wish the

Pilgrims ascending to the kever of Rabbi Shimon bar Yochai in Meron

Rebbe *Shalom Aleichem*, he pleaded with them tearfully, "Please allow me to enter quickly."

We were seized with fear and trepidation, for who could fathom the great holiness of this place that is the gravesite of the awesome Tanna Rabbi Shimon bar Yochai, about whom "Let us make man" was said. All of the creations of heaven and earth tremble at the utterances of his holy mouth, and many great earlier rabbanim were terrified to approach this tomb. What should we say!

But multitudes of Jews regularly enter the sanctuary, especially on the day of Lag BaOmer, and even great people are therefore not so particular about who enters to participate in the celebration. This gave us the courage to follow the Rebbe into the building's inner chamber, where the holy Tanna rests.

The building was illuminated with pure olive oil lamps, and innumerable candles were burning. There were people learning and reciting *Zohar* and *Tikkunei Zohar*; others were saying Tehillim, others were praying and reciting supplications; others were wearing tallis and tefillin and davening; some were playing musical instruments; and yet others were singing and praising Hashem. Some people were sitting low on the ground and occupying themselves with the aforementioned holy pursuits, while others were standing crowded together. There were also many people sleeping on the ground, exhausted from the exertion of the previous night.

British Governor (center, in dark suit) arrives in Meron to greet the Rebbe

There were also groups of people wearing festive clothing and dancing and clapping, rejoicing with their young sons who had gotten their first haircuts. They distributed whiskey and delicacies, wished each other *l'chaim* and blessed one another that they should raise their children to Torah. Whoever did not see this joy has never seen joy in his life. Overall, there was tremendous spiritual awakening. Fortunate is the nation for whom this is so.

All over Eretz Yisrael, and especially in Meron, the great significance of Lag BaOmer is acknowledged and recognized, at least somewhat. In the Diaspora, however, people are largely unaware of this, save for a few righteous and learned individuals.

The Rebbe approached the wall and the unusual, wide, smooth stone building, under which it is said that the cave of Rabbi Shimon bar Yochai is found. Tearfully, he learned and recited a few pages of *Idra Kadisha*. After that he read *kvitlach*, his lips murmuring with supplications for mercy for Klal Yisrael and for individuals. He also recited chapters of Tehillim.

All the people present experienced a spiritual awakening. After that, we donned tallis and tefillin and davened Shacharis in the inner sanctuary of the holy tomb.

While we were davening, the British governor of the Upper Galilee arrived to greet the Rebbe, and he waited until the prayers were over. It was said that the governor had acted kindly toward the Jews during the riots and massacres of 1929, and the Rebbe therefore received him cordially, with words of blessing.

The Rebbe blessed him that in the merit of the holy Tanna Rabbi Shimon bar Yochai, he should be rewarded in full for the kindnesses he performed for the Jews. He added that the governor should continue to be kind to the Jews, and thanked him for what he had done until now. The blessing was conveyed by the interpreter, and the governor responded cordially as well, thanking the Rebbe and displaying signs of honor. He then went on his way.

After davening, the Rebbe again approached the holy place opposite the cave and, with the people around him, he sang the *zemer* traditionally sung on Lag BaOmer: "*Bar Yochai, nimshachta ashrecha*" (Bar Yochai! You were anointed, you are fortunate) in the special tune. Pious people were dancing, with the Rebbe inside the circle, and everyone cried tears of joy as they sang and danced. How fortunate are we to have experienced this celebration.

After the dancing, the Rebbe told his followers humbly, "Do not be surprised that a simple person like me dared to dance and rejoice in this holy place before the Tanna Rabbi Shimon bar Yochai. I am relying on *zechus avos* (the merit of my ancestors), for I am the son of the great tzaddik who authored the *Be'er Lachai Ro'i* commentary on the *Tikkunei Zohar*. He undoubtedly merited a strong connection to the sanctuary of Rabbi Shimon bar Yochai, and as his son, I can rejoice in that merit as well."

RABBI ELUZAR, THE SON OF RABBI SHIMON BAR YOCHAI

Afterward, we again entered the large sanctuary of the ancient tomb. In the middle of that sanctuary, surrounded by an iron gate, is the grave of the great Tanna, Rabbi Eluzar the son of Rabbi Shimon. The Rebbe went inside the gate and raised his voice tearfully as he recited Tehillim. The people around him also poured out their hearts with excitement and trepidation, for on the day of his father's yahrtzeit, Rabbi Eluzar certainly had more power to arouse mercy for Klal Yisrael. Besides, we were awed by the exceptional holiness of Rabbi Eluzar, which instills fear in the hearts of those who approach his resting place.[1]

RABBI YITZCHAK

With feelings of longing, we left the holy sanctuary and entered the small cave near the outer gate where the holy Tanna Rabbi Yitzchak is buried. Rabbi Yitzchak was a member of Rabbi Shimon's exalted inner circle. In the holy *Zohar*, it is recorded that Rabbi Shimon bar Yochai went to great lengths to prevent Rabbi Yitzchak's passing, and caused his life to be extended. Rabbi Yitzchak's father came to his son from the next world in a dream to inform him of this, and told him how great a portion awaited him in Gan Eden. He also told Rabbi Yitzchak to prepare bread on the day of Rabbi Shimon's yahrtzeit. This saintly Tanna has infinite power to effect salvation with his prayers to Hashem on behalf of those who visit his tomb, and he is also one of those closest to Rabbi Shimon, standing and serving him in holiness.

It is uncertain whether Rabbi Yitzchak is buried inside the cave or outside. It is written in *Be'er Lachai Ro'i* that the members of Rabbi Shimon's inner circle, including Rabbi Yitzchak, were in the cave together with him when he was hiding, and there they composed the *Tikkunei Zohar*. According to this, in would appear that Rabbi Yitzchak experienced suffering in the cave and therefore could be buried with Rabbi Shimon bar Yochai inside the cave.

---

1. Rabbi Eluzar hid in the cave with his father, and the two learned Torah there for thirteen years, eating carobs and drinking water miraculously created for them (see *Shabbos* 33b). Also see *Sanhedrin* 97b, where Rabbi Shimon bar Yochai says that if there are two people of exalted caliber in the world, they are my son and me. Other great miracles involving Rabbi Eluzar are recorded in *Bava Metziah* 84, where it says that Rabbi Eluzar's body lay in an attic for over eighteen years after his death, and when people would come there for a *din Torah*, a Heavenly voice would emanate from the attic pronouncing which party was guilty and which was innocent. Eventually, one Erev Yom Kippur, the rabbis brought Rabbi Eluzar's body to the cave where his father was buried.

In the Gemara (*Bava Metzia* 84), however, it appears that the suffering experienced in the cave made one deserving of special merit. It is difficult to say that members of the inner circle, who did not have to flee from the Romans (as did Rabbi Shimon), voluntarily suffered by spending all those years in the cave with Rabbi Shimon. It is more likely that they came to the cave to learn with Rabbi Shimon only on occasion. If that is the case, it cannot be said that the inner circle experienced the same suffering as Rabbi Shimon, who spent thirteen years in the cave hiding from the government.

As for Rabbi Eluzar, the son of Rabbi Shimon bar Yochai, he did not have to be a fugitive from the Romans, but because he chose to be in the cave with his father the entire time, he is included in the suffering of the cave. If so, it is possible that the other students stayed in the cave continuously with Rabbi Shimon bar Yochai as well, accepting the suffering upon themselves because of their love of Torah, but it does not sound reasonable to say that. This matter needs further clarification.

If we assume that the Rabbi Yitzchak referred in the holy *Zohar* as a member of the inner circle of Rabbi Shimon bar Yochai is actually Rabbi Yitzchak Nafcha, then he is not the Rabbi Yitzchak who, according to Arizal, is buried in the cave in the courtyard of Rabbi Shimon bar Yochai, because Rabbi Yitzchak Nafcha's burial place is known to be far from the courtyard.

RABBI YOCHANAN HASANDLAR AND HILLEL AND SHAMMAI

From there, we went to the holy grave of the Tanna Rabbi Yochanan HaSandlar, who is also buried in Meron. His tomb is in a cave carved out of a mountain with a dome built above it. In a play on words, the Rebbe remarked, "We are now in the era of the 'Footsteps of Mashiach,' and we need a good shoemaker [*sandlar*, in Hebrew] to repair the heels of our shoes. Let us go, therefore, to Rabbi Yochanan HaSandlar, to daven at his grave and beg him to fix the heels."

Kever of Rabbi Yochanan HaSandlar

The Rebbe lit an oil lamp at the tomb of Rabbi Yochanan, and stayed there for a while saying Tehillim. May Rabbi Yochanan — who was also a student of Rabbi Akiva, like Rabbi Shimon bar Yochai — intercede favorably on our behalf.

On our way back from the grave of Rabbi Yochanan HaSandlar to the tomb of Rabbi Shimon bar Yochai, we stood with the Rebbe opposite the mountain where Hillel, Shammai, and their students are buried. From close up, it is possible to see crypts with coffins, but we stood at a distance. We said Tehillim and davened at the graves of these holy Tannaim, for each of whom the creation of the entire world was worthwhile.

RABBI YOSE B'RABBI YAAKOV AND THE PLACE OF THE IDRA

On the way from Meron to Tzefas, we stopped to daven in the field, at the base of the mountain, near a pile of stones marking the gravesite of the Tanna Rabbi Yose the son of Rabbi Yaakov, one of the students of Rabbi Shimon bar Yochai's royal court. Rabbi Yose is mentioned in *Idra Rabbah* in the holy *Zohar, Parashas Nasso*. He passed away with a Heavenly kiss at the time that the *Idra* was revealed, as explained at length in the *Idra*.

The field we were in was the holy field where Rabbi Shimon bar Yochai and his holy inner circle learned and composed the *Idra Rabbah*. The *Shaar HaGilgulim* of the Arizal records that Rabbi Shimon bar Yochai sat there, with Rabbi Eluzar and Rabbi Abba and others in close proximity. We merited visiting this awesome place with our holy Rebbe and reciting verses of supplication there.

RABBI YEHUDAH, THE SON OF RABBI ELA'I

On our way, we also davened at the tomb of the holy Tanna Rabbi Yehudah, the son of Rabbi Ela'i, who is buried in a cave deep in a mountain, in a crypt within a crypt.

Because the crypts are very low, it was not possible for the Rebbe to enter. Instead, he stood at the entrance to the cave dav-

Kever of Rabbi Yehudah ben Ela'i

ening and saying Tehillim. I, the lowly one, went inside, bending my head and my body and spreading my arms and legs, for it was impossible to enter upright. The Rebbe gave me *kvitlach* with names and requests written on them that he had found in his possession (from those that he had taken to the tomb of Rabbi Shimon bar Yochai in Meron) and told me, "Be an emissary of the Jewish people to leave [the *kvitlach*] inside the holy cave, and you will also be saved."

We were confident that the holy Tanna Rabbi Yehudah, the son of Rabbi Ela'i, who was known as "the head of the spokesmen for the Jewish people," would intercede favorably with Hashem on our behalf and on behalf of the entire Jewish people.

We continued on our way until we reached Tzefas.

THE CEMETERY IN TZEFAS

When we returned to Tzefas, exhausted from the day's exertion, it was already past midday on Friday, but the Rebbe specifically wished to daven on this day, Lag BaOmer, at the grave of the Arizal, who had illuminated the world by revealing the Torah of Rabbi Shimon bar Yochai. We quickly descended to the bottom of the large mountain, which is the ancient cemetery in Tzefas, to visit the holy graves found there.

First, we reached the grave of the head of the Kabbalists, the great and holy Arizal. The shape of his grave is similar to the graves in our country, housed in a dome of rocks approximately one cubit in height. The grave is covered with a stone inscribed with the name "Rabbeinu Yitzchak Luria Ashkenazi, deceased 5 Av 5332 at 38 years of age." Understandably, the excitement we felt at this grave was extraordinary, for the Arizal was a holy messenger sent from Heaven to illuminate future generations by revealing the wisdom of truth (Kabbalah). The Arizal saw, with his Divine inspiration, all the worlds from one end to the other, and the heavenly legions trembled from the words of his pure mouth. If a person were to come to the Holy Land only to daven at the grave of the Arizal, he would rejoice at his lot.

The Rebbe stood there and davened with holy thoughts and emotions. This was the tomb of the Arizal whose Torah he studied day and night, in the tradition of his holy forefathers, who had learned and transmitted the Torah of the Arizal from the holy Baal Shem Tov.

From the Arizal's grave, we proceeded to the nearby grave of the holy Rabbi Moshe Cordovero, the Ramak, who passed away on 23 Tammuz, 5330. His passing preceded that of the Arizal, and the Arizal escorted him to his final resting place, as recorded in *Ohr Tzaddikim* (by Rabbi Meir Papirsh). That work also describes in detail how two pillars of fire accompanied the Ramak's coffin. The Ramak is also buried under a dome, like the Arizal.

We also visited the grave of the holy Rabbi Shlomo Alkabetz, the teacher and brother-in-law of the Ramak. Rabbi Alkabetz was the author of the liturgical poem *Lecha Dodi*, and also authored *Manos HaLevi* on *Megillas Esther*. The Shelah HaKadosh writes that Rabbi Alkabetz was with the Beis Yosef during the revelation on the night of Shavuos.

The story is told in the holy Rabbi Shlomo ibn Gabirol's accounts of his travels in Eretz Yisrael that because of Rabbi Alkabetz's great

Yidden at the grave of Rav Shlomo Alkabetz in Tzefas

wisdom, the gentiles envied him, and an Arab killed him and buried him under a tree in his garden. When the tree bore fruit early, people investigated. The crime was discovered, and the murderer was hanged on that very tree. This story is recorded in the holy work *Kav HaYashar* (Chapter 86) about Rabbi Shlomo Alkabetz.

These three shepherds of the Jewish people, the holy angels mentioned above, are buried in close proximity to one another.

Not far from there is the grave of the holy Rabbi Yosef Karo, the author of the *Beis Yosef* and the *Shulchan Aruch*, whose decisive halachic rulings illuminate the revealed Torah for all generations. We prayed and recited verses of supplication at his grave.

How fortunate were we to have visited the graves of the giant of the hidden Torah — the Arizal — and the giant of the revealed Torah — the Beis Yosef. (Actually, both were learned in the hidden and revealed Torahs, but one taught the revealed Torah to future generations while the other taught the hidden Torah.)

On our way out of the cemetery, we stopped at the tomb of the Tanna Rabbi Pinchas ben Yair, who is buried in the field outside the Tzefas cemetery, and whose grave is surrounded by a pile of rocks. Rabbi Pinchas ben Yair was the father-in-law of Rabbi Shimon bar Yochai.

The Rebbe said that it is a tradition passed down from tzaddikim to perform *hakafah*-circuits at the grave of Rabbi Pinchas ben Yair, and we did so. The Rebbe walked at the head of the group reciting the verses of *Ana b'koach, Yosheiv b'seser*, etc. and we walked around the grave seven times. The spiritual awakening was intense, as we cried out and davened to Hashem, our tears falling freely on the holy stones of the tomb.

When we ascended from the mountain to the city of Tzefas, we passed the cave of the Tanna Rabbi Yehoshua. It is said that this is the grave of the prophet Hoshea ben Be'eiri, but the Rebbe quoted the Arizal who wrote explicitly (in *Shaar HaGilgulim*) that this is the grave of the Tanna Rabbi Yehoshua. From a distance, we poured out our hearts.

Because Shabbos was approaching, we could not visit any more graves on that day, even those whose locations we were aware of. (I myself went with the rabbanim of the group on Sunday morning to daven at these holy graves — the Alshich HaKadosh, Rabbi Yitzchak Abuhav, and the author of *Be'er Mayim Chaim* — and at graves of unknown tzaddikim. We also visited the cave of the Yanuka mentioned in the *Zohar* and the mikveh of the Arizal at the edge of the cemetery in Tzefas. We merited touching the mikveh's waters with our hands.)

When we left those tall mountains, the Rebbe told us that it is said in the name of the Arizal that on one mountain in Tzefas are buried twice the number of those who left Egypt.

After that, we arrived at our lodgings in Tzefas, exhausted from the exertion of this wonderful day. The Rebbe did not wish to depart from his custom of eating a *seudah* with his attentive followers on Lag BaOmer, so we quickly ate a *seudah* together in honor of the day.

At this point, the Rebbe received a telegram from Jerusalem asking him to daven for the Saba Kadisha. We were deeply pained by this information, but we strengthened ourselves with faith that the tzaddik would have a speedy recovery. After bentching, it was time to immerse in the mikveh in honor of Shabbos, for it was getting late.

CHAPTER 12

THE TENTH DAY

SHABBOS PARASHAS EMOR

When the holy Shabbos arrived, we went to the Sanzer Beis Medrash to daven. The congregants were wearing white and were wrapped in white talleisim draped over their heads, as we dress on Yom Kippur. The Rebbe davened Minchah for the *amud*, as was his custom.

In Tzefas, and in Teveriah as well, people do not daven toward the east, but toward the south, facing Jerusalem. When we said *Bo'i b'shalom*, therefore, we turned only to our right, facing westward, not all the way around as we normally do when davening eastward (based on the Talmud [*Bava Basra* 25b] which states that the *Shechinah* is in the west).

The *chazzan* for Maariv and Kabbalas Shabbos was a scholar from Jerusalem, one of the many who had joined the Rebbe in Tzefas, and the davening was beautiful in this congregation of chassidim and scholars. Before *K'gavna*, which is taken from R' Shimon bar

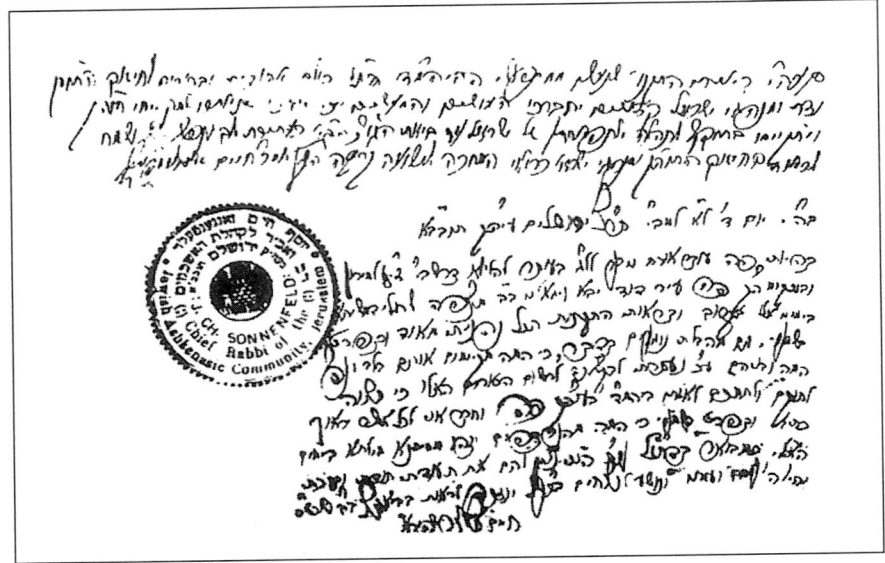

Letter of approbation written by the Rebbe for the Sanzer Shul in Tzefas

Yochai's *Zohar*, we sang the song *Bar Yochai*, as is customary in Tzefas. The singing was exceptionally meaningful on this day, after we had just merited visiting Rabbi Shimon bar Yochai's tomb on his yahrtzeit.

The *tisch* was held in the Sanzer Beis Medrash as well, and we spent the entire Shabbos in the company of the scholars of the holy city and its environs.

On Shabbos, everything was done as is customary in Jerusalem, except that the Kohanim recited the Priestly Blessing only during Mussaf, as is the Ashkenazi custom in Tzefas.

The Rebbe noted that the Ashkenazi custom in Jerusalem is that the Kohanim recite the Priestly Blessing daily, and twice on Shabbos. In other cities in Eretz Yisrael, the Priestly Blessing is recited only during Mussaf of Shabbos and Yom Tov, not during the week. (The Sephardic custom is different.) The Rebbe explained that the holy sources teach that the site of the Beis HaMikdash has great potential for holiness, and therefore equal potential for evil forces to take hold.

He showed us that the *Emes L'Yaakov*, authored by one of the early Sephardic greats, discusses this matter at length (*Maareches*

100, *Os* 38), noting that the inhabitants of the Holy City of Jerusalem need to be exceedingly careful to attach themselves to the forces of holiness. In Jerusalem, therefore, it is necessary to recite the Priestly Blessing every day, to negate the forces of impurity and arouse Heavenly blessing and favor.

A Bris Milah with the Sephardim

After davening, we went to the beis medrash of the Sephardim for a *bris milah*. The Rebbe was honored to act as both *sandek* and *mohel*, and a large crowd gathered in his honor in the streets of Tzefas. Once again, we enjoyed hearing the Sephardic *nusach* and the verses they recite when the baby is brought to the beis medrash.

The congregation and the other townspeople who had gathered — both Ashkenazim and Sephardim — stood and watched from inside and outside as the Rebbe performed the mitzvah with alacrity and skill.

The blessing *Asher kiddash yedid* was recited by a Sephardic chacham, an outstanding scholar, who was also a Kohen. The Rebbe was told that this chacham was the son of a holy tzaddik whom the Shiniver Rav had known, and he asked the chacham to bless him with the Priestly Blessing. He did so, and the Rebbe blessed him, with love and admiration.

After that, we returned to our lodgings and to the Sanzer Beis Medrash for Kiddush and the Shabbos day *seudah*, which we ate together with a large crowd.

The Shul and Sefer Torah of Rabbi Yitzchak Abuhav

After the *seudah*, the Rebbe did not sleep, for he strongly desired to read from the *Sefer Torah* of Rabbi Yitzchak Abuhav. The Rebbe had spoken and inquired about this *Sefer Torah* throughout our journey on the ship, and had continued speaking about it here in Tzefas.

He made his way to the holy shul, whose origin is traced back to the saintly Rabbi Yitzchak Abuhav.[1] We were awed by this spacious, beautiful shul, and the Rebbe davened Minchah for the *amud* with obvious emotion.

When the *Aron Kodesh* was opened, the ancient *Sefer Torah* was removed. Usually, it was read from only on a few special occasions

The Abuhav Shul in Tzefas

---

1. It is uncertain whether it was he or his grandfather who authored the *Menoras HaMaor*.

during the year, but in honor of the Rebbe, it was removed now as well, and handled with fear and trepidation.

In keeping with the Sephardic custom, the *Sefer Torah* was contained in a round, closed case. Before reading from the Torah, they raised it for *hagba'ah*, turning the script in all directions, and then putting it down to be read. (This is the custom in the Holy City of Jerusalem, as well, before the Torah reading.)

The *Sefer Torah* was placed upright in its case on the *bimah*. The case was opened, and the script was read with the Torah standing straight up. How delightful it was to see the pure, holy letters of this ancient scroll! Fortunate is the eye that witnessed this, and fortunate is the ear that heard the Rebbe reading the first portion of *Parashas Behar*. The Rebbe also had the third *aliyah*, inspiring fear and awe in all those who heard him recite the blessings.

THE ARIZAL'S SHUL

We proceeded from there to the holy shul traced back to the Arizal, also a large, imposing building. Inside the shul, at the side, there is a low, cave-like room with a special rock, where tradition has it that Elijah the Prophet appeared to the Arizal. That was also where the Arizal sat.

It is recorded in the holy sources that once, the Arizal was reading the Torah in his shul, and he called up Aharon for the Kohen *aliyah*, Moshe for the Levi *aliyah*, Avraham for the third *aliyah*, Yitzchak for the fourth *aliyah*, Yaakov for the fifth *aliyah*, Yosef for the sixth *aliyah*, etc.

We entered this holy place with fear and awe. The Rebbe seated himself low on the stoop at the entrance to the cave with the holy stone, and learned the fourth chapter of *Pirkei Avos* there in an emotional voice. After kissing the stones and earth we left, for the sun was setting and it was time to eat *seudah shelishis*.

We passed by the holy ruins of Tzefas, which ruthless Arabs had destroyed the previous year, when they massacred Jews without mercy. We were shown the ruins of a house where the Arabs' first victim, a great rabbi and scholar, had lived. They fell upon this scholar while he was learning Torah and murdered him in cold blood. These sights shook us deeply; may Hashem avenge the blood of the innocent.

THE TIME OF INTENSE HEAVENLY FAVOR

For *seudah shelishis*, the Rebbe had decided to eat only in his house, not in the Sanzer Beis Medrash. He did not want the congregants to change the customary *zemiros* and verses they recited according to the tradition of the holy Rebbe of Sanz, but he also did not want to depart from his own custom passed down from the holy Rabbi Tzvi Elimelech of Dinov, the author of the *Bnei Yissas'char*. But the congregants prevailed upon him not to leave their beis medrash at this aus-picious time, and they left it to him to do as he wished, as though it were his own beis medrash. They felt that by departing from their custom now, and permitting the Rebbe to follow his tradition, they would elevate themselves spiritually, and thus strengthen themselves in the future. They said that members of the congregation who did not wish to change their custom were free to say their own *nusach* quietly, to themselves.

The Rebbe

Finally, the Rebbe acquiesced, and went to the beis medrash for *seudah shelishis*. The great leaders and scholars of Tzefas and other holy cities who were there for Shabbos joined us in that holy place at that time of intense Heavenly favor.

When it was time to say *divrei Torah*, trepidation seized all those present, for the Rebbe uttered holy, fiery words of *mussar*. He raised the issue of the breaches that had been made by the Zionists and their ilk, particularly in Tzefas, in the area of education.

"Have mercy, my beloved brothers," the Rebbe said with bitter tears, "on yourselves, on your sons and daughters, and on the entire Jewish people. Stand up against them and raise the flag of Torah [by adhering to] the traditional education, in the purity of holiness."

The Rebbe roared like a lion, crying out, "How can they not be concerned for their souls, especially in this holy city of Tzefas, the home of the author of the *Shulchan Aruch*! [How can they] disobey the rulings of the rabbi of the city, violating rabbinic and Torah prohibitions? The light of the holy Beis Yosef still shines, and his honor lies here in the cemetery, as do great luminaries such as the Radvaz, the Arizal, the Alshich, the Ramak and others. These lofty angels stand before you, watching your conduct from their resting places here, and their power and righteousness remain forever. How dare people desecrate their holy place by straying from their path, the path of Hashem and the Torah! Therefore, please, my brothers, guard your souls and take care that you should not be burnt in this terrible fire. Rather, heed the Torah passed down from Mount Sinai, and you will thereby hasten the ultimate redemption. For those who obey, it will be good. You will be blessed, and the merit of our holy teachers will help you and protect you."

These words penetrated the hearts of all those listening, and everyone shed tears of repentance.

Prior to *Bircas HaMazon* of *seudah shlishis*, the Rebbe sat with those present and talked about the holy angels of Tzefas who illuminated the entire world. He bemoaned the fact that no one knows the location of the graves of many of these giants, such as the

Radvaz,[2] who learned Torah frequently from Elijah the Prophet; the author of the *Mikdash Melech*;[3] the author of the *Chareidim*;[4] the Mabit;[5] Mahari bei Rav;[6] and innumerable others. It is known that these rabbanim are buried in Tzefas, but because the exact location of their resting places is unknown, it is impossible to pray at their graves. The Rebbe extolled the praises of these great individuals, of whose greatness we can comprehend but a drop in the ocean.

During these discussions, he told a remarkable story that he heard from his holy grandfather Rabbi Shlomo Shapira, who heard it from his father-in-law, Rabbi Shmelke of Sassov, who heard it from an elderly sage in Tzefas. This sage read the story in a handwritten manuscript on *Maseches Shabbos* written by the saintly Rabbi Sar Shalom Buzaglo, author of the *Mikdash Melech* on

Tombstone of the holy Rebbe of Sassov, Rav Yekusiel Shmelke, in Jagolnice, Ukraine

2. Rabbeinu David ibn Zimra, who taught much Torah and had many great students. He wrote over 2000 halachic rulings, of which only 300 were printed.
3. Rabbeinu Sar Shalom Buzaglo, the son of Rabbi Moshe from the city of Sali. He was the closest student of Rabbi Avraham Azulai in the study of Kabbalah.
4. Rabbeinu Eluzar Azikri, who passed away around the year 5361/1601.
5. Rabbeinu Moshe di Trani, born in Salonika in the year 5265/1505.
6. Rabbeinu Yaakov, known as Bei Rav. He was the rebbi of the Mabit.

the holy *Zohar*. In the introduction to his work on *Maseches Shabbos*, the *Mikdash Melech* recorded a story that had happened to him. He was traveling by ship from London to the holy city of Tzefas, and on Friday, the ship docked at a port along the way. Many of the passengers, among them the *Mikdash Melech*, left the ship for a short while.

Absorbed in profound thoughts, he strolled alone and wandered off into the nearby forest. When he realized that he had strayed far from the ship, he quickly made his way back to where the ship had docked. To his dismay, he found that it had already sailed with all its passengers, leaving him alone in this unpopulated area.

He returned to where he had been in the forest, and realized that it was almost sundown, and that Shabbos was fast approaching.

From a distance, he noticed what seemed to be a building and a wall in the forest. He was unsure whether to make his way there, for fear that the building was inhabited by bandits or murderers.

Suddenly, he saw a large eagle flying toward him. It landed on the ground near him and spread out its large wings, as though beckoning him to climb aboard. He gingerly stood on the eagle's wings, and the eagle carried him to the very building he had been looking at, deposited him there, and flew off.

The *Mikdash Melech* found himself standing outside an imposing, beautiful palace. His heart pounding, he pushed open the door and entered one room after another. There was no one inside.

The palace contained halls of ivory decorated with precious stones, gold-plated pillars, and exquisite utensils of silver and gold, fit for a king. The *Mikdash Melech* was astounded by this incredible sight, and marveled at the way Hashem had led him here to find refuge. Now, he knew that he did not have to worry, for he realized that he was in *Gan Eden*. All he needed to do was to call out to Hashem.

Addressing his Creator, he said, "My custom has always been to immerse myself in a mikveh on Erev Shabbos in honor of Shabbos." As he was speaking, he raised his eyes and noticed a mikveh in a different room. He immersed himself in the mikveh and washed his hands. Then he said, "My custom has always been to wear four white garments in honor of the holy Shabbos." Immediately, he noticed four white garments lying before him. Then he said, "My custom has always been to learn *Maseches Shabbos* on Shabbos, and to begin learning in the afternoon, as Shabbos enters." Instantly, there was a beautiful Gemara *Shabbos* in front of him. Finally, he said, "My custom has always been to taste the Shabbos food on Erev Shabbos," and on the table before him appeared a dish with fine fish. He tasted the fish, then seated himself at the table dressed in the white garments and began learning from the Gemara. As he pored over the Gemara, many extraordinary *chiddushim* on *Maseches Shabbos* entered his mind.

Soon, he noticed a beautiful candelabrum on the table with candles and a flame to light the candles. He saw that the sun would soon set, and he lit the candles in honor of Shabbos.

Suddenly, he heard noises coming from an inner room. It sounded as though people were entering and gathering. Tentatively, he tried to open the door of the inner room, but he was unable to. He understood that he was not authorized to enter, and he returned to his place.

He heard the people in the inner room beginning to daven Minchah, and he donned a tallis and davened with them in awe and fear. After the Friday night prayers were over, the inner chamber fell silent, and he sat quietly in his own chamber watching as challah, meat, fish, and other delicacies appeared on the table. He enjoyed these other-worldly delicacies, recited *Bircas HaMazon*, and then went to sleep on the bed that had been prepared for him.

On Shabbos morning he again immersed in the mikveh. For a second time, he sensed that a holy crowd was gathering in the inner room, and he davened with them from his room. During the reading of the Torah, he heard the seven shepherds — Avraham, Yitzchak, Yaakov, etc., all the way to King David — being called to the Torah. He was seized with fear and awe, realizing that he was indeed in *Gan Eden*.

When davening was over, he found a *seudah* prepared for him as on the previous night. The entire day, he learned *Maseches Shabbos*, and he also napped in the afternoon.

Later, he davened Minchah with the congregants in the inner chamber, and then washed his hands for *seudah shelishis*. He ate the fish prepared for him and sang *Askinu Seudasa* and other *zemiros*.

Toward evening, as Shabbos was departing, he felt overcome by fatigue, even though he had slept at night and during the day. He did not wish to fall asleep in the middle of the *seudah*, so he quickly washed *mayim acharonim* and recited *Bircas HaMazon*. As soon as he finished *Bircas HaMazon*, before he even had a change to lie down on the bed, slumber overtook him and he fell asleep at the table.

He dreamt that he was in an upper world, in the place where the Heavenly Court sits. Now, at the conclusion of Shabbos, the court was passing judgment on those souls that had passed away during Shabbos. In his vision, he watched as the court deliberated the judgment of a number of departed souls. When it was announced that a certain soul was a tzaddik, there was a joyous tumult in heaven, and the Heavenly legions made place in Gan Eden.

Among those souls undergoing judgment was an elderly man, about 80 years old, who had passed away on Shabbos. This man had owned a tavern near the holy city of Tzefas. When the court judged him, it was announced that he was a tzaddik and could enter Gan Eden. All of a sudden, a black, frightening-looking angel appeared and shouted, "Wait! Wait with this old man from the village near Tzefas, for I know of a flaw in him. Once, an Arab came to his tavern on Shabbos and asked him to sell him a certain drink. The man did not want to sell him the drink because it was Shabbos, but the Arab threatened that if he did not give it to him, he would be killed. The man told the Arab to take the drink from the tavern himself, and the Arab took it and left. In doing so, this man gave at least the appearance of a possible Shabbos prohibition, and how can he be allowed to enter Gan Eden?"

The Heavenly court convened to consider the angel's allegation. One angel defended the man, arguing that he had not taken any payment for the drink and that he had been forced to do what he did because his life was in danger. Nevertheless, the court ruled that although the man was a Torah scholar and a tzaddik, he had caused a blemish on his soul according to the view of *Tosafos* (*Maseches Shabbos* 3a בתוד"ה בבא דרישא). Because he was guilty of appearing to violate a Rabbinic prohibition, his soul would have to wander for seven years. Through this, the blemish on his soul would be rectified, and afterward he could enter Gan Eden.

When the *Mikdash Melech* heard this ruling, he was bewildered. Even the judgment of evildoers is only twelve months; why should a righteous individual like this old man be given seven years of severe punishment for something that was only a trace of a sin? He had tremendous pity on the old man, and he could not hold himself back, so he presented himself before the Heavenly court and said, "I wish to offer my soul instead of this man's, and I accept upon myself to suffer seven years of wandering instead of him. Let him go to Gan Eden."

The court agreed to this suggestion and freed the old man from his punishment. The old man bowed his head in an expression of thanks to the *Mikdash Melech*, and he was led immediately to Gan Eden.

After that, a voice emanated from the Heavenly Court announcing that they would begin to consider the judgment of the *Mikdash Melech*, who had accepted upon himself with great self-sacrifice a severe punishment, out of love for a Jew whom he never knew and had never met. In doing so, they said, he had fulfilled a great mitzvah; why should he be punished?

The court ruled that the punishment should be eased, and that one day should be reckoned as a full year of punishment. It was decided that instead of seven years, the *Mikdash Melech* would have to wander for only seven days.

The old man who passed away had seven sons. It was decreed that the *Mikdash Melech* should sleep one night at the home of each of the sons, and the Heavenly Court would consider it as though he had wandered for seven years. After that, he would be able to enjoy the good of the Holy Land for many long years.

The *Mikdash Melech* awoke and saw that he was sitting in a field, with no palace, no rooms, no table, no utensils — nothing. Suddenly, from a distance, he noticed that a large crowd of people was approaching, holding lanterns to illuminate the area. When they reached him, he asked them where he was, and he was told that he was in the holy city of Tzefas, and the mountain on which he was standing was a cemetery.

The people asked him who he was and where he was from, but he avoided their questions. Instead, he asked them why they were coming here in the middle of the night. They answered that on the

Shabbos that had just passed, a respected, 80-year-old Torah scholar had passed away. Several hours after Shabbos, they had escorted him to his final resting place in the Tzefas cemetery, and they were now returning to their homes.

The *Mikdash Melech* realized that he had been carried from afar by Heaven to Tzefas, where he had desired to live. He stood, shaken, recalling the vision he had seen and marveling at the way every detail of the vision was unfolding before his eyes.

He did not tell the people what had happened, only that he was a Torah student and that he was unfamiliar with his surroundings and had nowhere to sleep.

The old man's seven sons were among the group, and they each asked him to come to their respective homes to sleep. He answered, "Please do not argue because of me. I will fulfill all of your wishes, G-d willing, by sleeping one night at each of your homes."

That is what happened, and that is how the *Mikdash Melech* discharged the judgment that he had accepted upon himself in the vision. Later, it became known in Tzefas that he was a holy man, and he lived there until his passing.

The *Mikdash Melech* related this entire story in the introduction to his work on *Maseches Shabbos*. He wrote there that he thought of most of his novellae on that tractate during the Shabbos that he spent in the Heavenly Gan Eden, tasting from the Tree of Knowledge. May the merit of the holy *Mikdash Melech* protect us and the entire Jewish people.

The Rebbe also told a story related by the holy Shiniver Rav, which he heard from a reliable source in Tzefas during his visit to the Holy Land. The story was about Rabbi Eluzar Azikri, the author of the *Sefer Chareidim*, who lived at the time of the Beis Yosef, the Arizal, and the Alshich. Rabbi Eluzar was the sexton in the beis medrash in Tzefas, and no one was aware of his great holiness. They took him to be a simpleton.

Once, on Lag BaOmer, the Arizal and his students were dancing at the holy tomb of Rabbi Shimon bar Yochai in Meron. There was a tall, striking Sephardic old man there, dressed in white, standing head and shoulders above the rest of the crowd. This old man danced with great joy, alone, and also together with a group of his peers, whom they did not recognize. At one point during the dancing, the old man danced with Rabbi Eluzar. Then the Arizal jumped up and grasped the hand of the old man and the two danced together for a long time. After that the Arizal took the hand of Rabbi Eluzar the sexton, and they danced with him, as well, for a long time.

After they left, some of the students of the Arizal mustered the courage to ask their teacher to explain what they had seen. "Our master danced with the old sage whom we did not recognize, for surely he is a great man. But why

Drawing of the holy Rebbe, Rav Yecheskel Shraga Halberstam of Shiniva

did his honor dance with Rabbi Eluzar Azikri, who is merely a sexton? It is not befitting the honor of the teacher of all of Israel to dance with him alone."

When the Arizal heard this, he laughed. "If the holy Tanna Rabbi Shimon bar Yochai danced alone with him, is it not befitting for me, the small one, to dance with him?" he replied. The students understood then that the old man they had seen had been none other than Rabbi Shimon bar Yochai, and they realized how great and holy the simple sexton really was.

CHAPTER 13

THE ELEVENTH DAY

THE SHUL IN TEVERIAH

The next day, Sunday, we left Tzefas and headed for the holy city of Teveriah. When we arrived, we found a large crowd waiting for us, and the Rebbe asked them to show him the way to the shul where the Arizal had davened. The Arizal had said, with Divine Inspiration (*Ruach HaKodesh*), that this shul had tremendous sanctity.

We davened Shacharis in this holy shul, and the Rebbe stood close to the Arizal's designated spot in the shul's northwest corner. We touched and kissed that holy spot, as well. A group of Sephardic scholars and their chacham came to this shul (which was a Sephardic shul) to greet the Rebbe.

Near this shul is a chassidic beis medrash where the saintly disciples of the Baal Shem Tov had prayed. These disciples were Rabbi Avraham of Kalisk (his designated spot was in the southwest corner); Rabbi Yaakov Shimshon of Shpetivka (his designated spot was in the northwest corner); and Rabbi Zev Wolf of Charny-Osra'ah. We entered the beis medrash and the Rebbe spoke holy words. In addition, stories were told about the greatness of these tzaddikim.

Rabbi Meir Baal Haness and Somchus his Disciple

From there, we traveled to the tomb of Rabbi Meir Baal Haness, which overlooks the Kinneret. Above this gravesite there is a beis medrash. The Rebbe offered a mystical explanation as to why there are no batei medrash or yeshivos on graves of other Tannaim and Amoraim, only on that of Rabbi Meir Baal Haness.

We entered the inner cave and were seized with trepidation. Rabbi Meir Baal Haness is the Tanna to whom we refer when we call out: *"Eloka d'Meir aneina* — G-d of Meir, answer me." The Gemara (*Avodah Zarah* 18) relates that Rabbi Meir once told a prison officer that at a time of distress he should say *"Eloka d'Meir aneina."* It has been a Jewish tradition since ancient times that when a person do-

The tomb of Rabbi Meir Baal Haness in Teveriah

nates money to the Rabbi Meir Baal Haness fund and says *"Eloka d'Meir aneina,"* he is assured that salvation will come speedily from Heaven.

We davened and said Tehillim at his holy grave, hoping to arouse Heavenly mercy, for the power of Rabbi Meir Baal Haness is great. About Rabbi Meir the Sages said that even in a generation of knowledge such as his there is none like him (see *Eruvin* 13b). Just as Rabbi Meir illuminated the eyes of the Sages in halachah, may he likewise illuminate our eyes.

Near Rabbi Meir's grave is the grave of his disciple Somchus. The Sages said (ibid.) in praise of Somchus that he expounded for every item of *tumah* 48 reasons for its being *tamei*, and for every item of ritual purity 48 reasons that it should be ritually pure. We davened that he should intercede favorably on our behalf and on behalf of the entire Jewish people.

On his way out of the tomb of Rabbi Meir Baal Haness, the Rebbe acquiesced to the request of the students of the yeshivah and beis medrash to visit their sanctuary. This yeshivah was called Yeshivah Ohr HaTorah, and its leader was Rabbi Moshe Kliers. Delicacies were served in the Rebbe's honor, and he agreed to write a warm

The Rebbe being escorted out of the tomb of Rabbi Meir Baal Haness by Rav Moshe Kliers

and eloquent recommendation to encourage donors to contribute to the beis medrash and yeshivah. We parted from them lovingly.

RABBI YIRMIYAH

From there, we made our way to the bottom of the mountain, at the side of the road, where Rabbi Yirmiyah is buried. This was the Rabbi Yirmiyah who believed so strongly in the principle of "I await the Mashiach's arrival every day" that he asked to be buried with his staff in his hand, lying on his side, so that he could stand up the moment Mashiach arrives (see *Yerushalmi, Kilayim* Ch. 9).

There is a pile of stones on top of and around Rabbi Yirmiyah's grave, which is surrounded by an iron barrier. We stood with the Rebbe at this holy site, reciting Tehillim to arouse Heavenly mercy.

We passed the healing waters of the hot springs of Teveriah, but because we had a trip ahead of us we did not stop there (except for a few members of the group who did bathe there). In addition, the Rebbe did not wish to enjoy those waters. (See *Pesachim* 8, where it is written that the reason these hot springs are not located in

The Rebbe and chassidim praying at the grave of Rabbi Yirmiyah in Teveriah

Jerusalem is so that the pilgrims should not say, "Had we come here only to bathe in these hot springs it would have been worthwhile," rendering their motives for the pilgrimage impure.)

We were also shown the location of the well of Miriam in the Kinneret (see *Shabbos* 35a, and *Rashi, Bamidbar* 21:20), and the place where the Arizal immersed himself in the Kinneret.

THE STUDENTS OF THE BAAL SHEM TOV

Next, we traveled to the cemetery in Teveriah to visit the graves of the saintly tzaddikim, the disciples of the Baal Shem Tov and his holy colleagues. These tzaddikim were Rabbi Yaakov Shimshon of Shpetivka, who passed away on 3 Sivan 5561/1801; Rabbi Nachman of Horodenka, who passed away on 2 Iyar 5548/1788 (Rabbi Yaakov Shimshon and Rabbi Nachman share one long tombstone); and the holy Rabbi Avraham of Kalisk, who passed away on 4 Shevat 5570/1810, as well as his disciples. All of these tzaddikim are buried in the same vicinity.

The Rebbe inquired as to the whereabouts of the grave of the holy Rabbi Avraham Yehoshua Heschel (the Apta Rav, author of *Oheiv Yisrael*) who passed away in Mezhibuzh on 5 Nissan 5585/1825 and was reburied in the holy city of Teveriah. We were shown the tombstone in the cemetery that marks the place where he is said to be buried.

RABBAN YOCHANAN BEN ZAKKAI

We traveled to the city's outer limits and entered a courtyard enclosed by a fence, where the great Tanna Rabban Yochanan ben Zakkai and other Tannaim and Amoraim are buried. We entered this holy courtyard, and the first grave we encountered was that of the Shelah HaKadosh, Rabbi Yeshayah Segal Horowitz.

The Shelah immigrated to the Holy City of Jerusalem in the year 5382/1622. He experienced much suffering there, and later settled in Teveriah; it was there that he was buried.

When the Rebbe learned that he was at the gravesite of the Shelah, he was seized with trepidation and fear. He told us that the Shelah was the progenitor of his family's *yichus*, since his mother was descended from the Ropshitzer Rebbe, whose family was traced back to the Shelah HaKadosh. He then davened with us at that holy gravesite.

Afterward, we approached the grave of the great Rabban Yochanan ben Zakkai, one of the early Tannaim who lived at the time of the Beis HaMikdash. Rabban Yochanan ben Zakkai was the teacher of Rabbi Eliezer HaGadol and of Rabbi Akiva, who in turn was the teacher of Rabbi Shimon bar Yochai.

Tradition has it that Rabban Yochanan ben Zakkai's great disciples are buried near him. These are the five great students discussed in *Pirkei Avos*, one of whom is Rabbi Eliezer ben Horkanus (Rabbi Eliezer HaGadol). However, the Rebbe expressed doubt that Rabbi Eliezer is actually buried there, referring to the Gemara in *Sanhedrin* (68a) which states that Rabbi Eliezer HaGadol passed away on Erev Shabbos, and on Motza'ei Shabbos, when Rabbi Akiva saw his coffin being carried from Caesarea to Lod, he hit his flesh until his blood flowed freely onto the ground. This Gemara seems to indicate that Rabbi Eliezer is not buried in Teveriah. The other disciples of Rabban Yochanan ben Zakkai are, apparently, buried there and we merited davening at their graves.

There are another two graves there that are said to be the graves of the Kohanim, Rabbi Ami and Rabbi Assi.

THE RAMBAM AND HIS FATHER

Inside the aforementioned fence there is a large, ornate gate that opens to the gravesites of the Rambam and his father. These graves are housed in a beautiful building with marble on the outside (on the large gate) and on the inside (on the wall) inscribed with the words, "Here lies Rabbeinu Moshe ben Maimon, the finest of humanity, about whom the scholars of his generation said, 'From Moshe to Moshe there was none like Moshe.'" The inscription also says, "The

The Rebbe walking through the gate at the kever of the Rambam

Rambam was born on 14 Nissan 4895 / 1135, and he passed away on 20 Teves 4965 / 1204."

The Rambam is the teacher of all the Jewish people who drink from the well of his Torah. We merited approaching and touching his holy grave, which is topped by a tall, wide dome covered in plaster. The Rambam's father, Rabbeinu Maimon, is also buried there (as the Arizal wrote at the end of *Shaar HaGilgulim*).

The Rebbe became very angry when he saw that besides the words inscribed in *lashon hakodesh*, the marble stones marking the grave of the Rambam (on the gate outside and at the entrance to the tomb) were also inscribed with the secular dates of his birth and death: 30 March 1135 — 13 December 1204. These impure words were inscribed by travelers who did not recognize Hashem or follow his Torah.

When he saw these words, the Rebbe immediately acted for the honor of the Torah and the honor of the great Rambam and scribbled over the offending dates with a pencil, as far as he could reach. He wrote on the stone in his holy handwriting that the Torah forbids writing in the language of the gentiles on Jewish tombstones (as explained in *Teshuvos Maharam Schick*), even on the tombstones of simple people, and especially on the grave of a man of G-d like the Rambam.

The Rebbe expressed his objection to the people from Teveriah who were with us, appointing them his agents to approach the rabbanim and community leaders of Teveriah who were in a position to rectify this matter and beg them to see to it that the inscriptions of the passersby be removed. He added that people do not realize how terrible it is to desecrate the holy place where a man of G-d is buried.

(Later, when the Rebbe returned to Jerusalem, he discussed this matter with the Saba Kadisha. Following the Saba's advice, he wrote to the Ashkenazi and Sephardic rabbanim in Teveriah.)

The Rebbe's efforts were successful; after a few months the rabbanim sent a letter to his home to notify him that they were able to

The Rebbe with the rabbanim of Teveriah

rectify the wrongdoing. They removed the stone with the foreign writing from the Rambam's gravesite, leaving only the marble inscribed in *lashon hakodesh*.

RABBI AKIVA AND HIS DISCIPLES

We left that holy area and headed toward the mountain where the saintly Tanna Rabbi Akiva is buried. Just hearing his holy name inspires fear and awe, and seeing the mountain where he is buried certainly does.

Rabbi Akiva had tens of thousands of great disciples, among them Rabbi Shimon bar Yochai, and his Torah illuminates the world until the end of generations. Even before the giving of the Torah, Hashem told Moshe Rabbeinu that Rabbi Akiva is destined to expound numerous halachos on the crowns of every letter in the Torah (*Menachos* 29). In addition, things that were not revealed to Moshe were revealed to Rabbi Akiva (*Midrash Rabbah, Parashas Chukas*).

It was not possible for us to go all the way to Rabbi Akiva's grave, because it is surrounded by large rocks and boulders. It was difficult for us to climb to the top of the mountain, especially after the exertion of the day up until this point. It was also around the time of *Minchah Ketanah*, and the sun was beating down on us. Moreover, we were anxious to get back to Jerusalem to find out how the Saba Kadisha was. We therefore contented ourselves with merely seeing Rabbi Akiva's grave and davening from afar.

A group of great rabbanim did ascend the mountain to Rabbi Akiva's grave, and the Rebbe asked one of them to mention his name at the holy site and daven that he should merit success in his endeavors, and that the requests of his heart be fulfilled to bring about salvation and redemption speedily.

At the base of the mountain where Rabbi Akiva is buried is the tomb of Rabbi Chiyya and his sons.

With this, we completed our visits to the graves of tzaddikim. In their merit, may Hashem fulfill all of the requests of our hearts for the good. May they all intercede favorably on our behalf, and may they all awaken to see the joy of the redemption.

Grave of Rabbi Akiva in Teveriah

The heat was overpowering, especially at that time when the sun was at its zenith. We still had a long day ahead of us, and we needed to rest before heading back to Jerusalem. We stopped at the house of a certain Torah scholar, where we davened Minchah and ate a bit. By then, it was already 4 o'clock, and we had to begin our return trip to Jerusalem.

We arrived in the Holy City at about 9 p.m., and went straight to the Saba Kadisha's house, even before going back to our lodgings. We were very disturbed to find him in a weakened state due to his illness.

He strengthened himself in his bed and asked the Rebbe if he had been to Teveriah and Meron and Tzefas. He inquired further about the Rebbe's trip, and the Rebbe answered him.

Afterward, the Rebbe asked the Saba Kadisha's attendant in German about his condition and his illness. The attendant replied that the doctor was very pessimistic and suspected that the Saba Kadisha had a lung infection. Both of them thought that the Saba Kadisha did not understand German, but it seemed that he understood everything, for he reprimanded the attendant, "Why are you speaking like that?"

Apparently, the Saba Kadisha did not wish to cause the Rebbe distress. We saw with our own eyes how he loved the Rebbe like a son, and when he spoke to him he always used affectionate terms: "I know, my son," "Sit, my son," and "Tell me, my son." The Rebbe considered it an honor when the Saba Kadisha addressed him in the second person and called him "my son," especially because it was known that the Saba Kadisha did not flatter anyone. For his part, the Rebbe always answered the Saba Kadisha using honorific terms, addressing him with such titles as "his holy eminence."

The Rebbe did not wish to impose on the Saba Kadisha too much, and we therefore did not stay long. We left, distressed over his condition.

CHAPTER 14

THE TWELFTH DAY

THE SABA KADISHA'S ILLNESS

The following day, Monday, I was sent by the Rebbe to inquire as to the Saba Kadisha's well-being. When I arrived at the Saba Kadisha's house, I asked, in the Rebbe's name, about his health. He responded, "Good, good!" He then told me to convey his request that the Rebbe visit that day, for he wished to speak with him privately.

The Sephardic Jew who transcribed the Saba Kadisha's writings from Sephardic script to the traditional Hebrew script began showing me and telling me about the *haskamah* that the Saba Kadisha had written the night before for the Rebbe's holy works. (The Rebbe had asked the Saba Kadisha for this *haskamah* prior to our trip.). However, the Saba Kadisha motioned to him that he should not speak too much, but rather perform his work diligently. I immediately retreated and took leave of the Saba Kadisha. When I returned to the Rebbe, I told him what had happened and relayed the Saba Kadisha's words.

In the afternoon, I went with the Rebbe to the Saba Kadisha's home. I remained in the outer room, and the Rebbe entered the sickroom. The Saba Kadisha asked him to sit next to the bed, and happily presented his *haskamah*. (This letter appears in *Minchas Eluzar*, Volume 4.) The two continued to converse for a very long time, but their voices could not be heard outside the room.

On the previous Thursday, before our trip to Meron, the Rebbe had given the Saba Kadisha *kvitlach* with the customary *pidyon* donation, from people who had asked him to give them to the tzaddik. The Saba Kadisha had accepted the *kvitlach* and had placed them under his pillow. Now, he returned two of them along with the *pidyon* money to the Rebbe. The Rebbe prevailed upon him to accept the *kvitlach* and pray for the people who had sent them, but he agreed to take only one of them back. He also refused to keep the money, instructing the Rebbe to distribute it to charity.

The Rebbe was astounded, and observed that after the Saba Kadisha had read the name on the *kvittel*, he had understood, with Divine Inspiration, what type of person this was. Nothing more need be said.

The Saba Kadisha did not make any mention of his illness. When the Rebbe inquired as to his health, he said, "Good." The Rebbe received his parting blessing, and wished him a speedy recovery, to which the Saba Kadisha replied, "Amen." Then we left. It did not occur to us that this was the last time the Saba Kadisha would speak to the Rebbe at length.

We did not have the peace of mind to visit other holy places on that day. Some time was set aside for people who wished to come speak to the Rebbe and hear his holy words and advice.

On that day, toward evening, Dr. Moshe Wallach, who attended

Doctor Moshe Wallach (left)

to the Saba Kadisha,[1] came to the Rebbe's lodgings to consult with him. He informed the Rebbe that the Saba Kadisha was suffering from a lung infection, and added that in his opinion, the condition was critical. It was decided to put leeches on the Saba Kadisha's holy body, in the hope that Hashem would heal his illness.

"The Saba Kadisha's illness is beyond our comprehension," the Rebbe commented. "At his age [approximately 120], his life is not in the realm of the natural; how can we attempt to heal him with natural means?"

The Rebbe added that searching for a cure is analogous to a midwife looking for medication when the Matriarch Sarah was giving birth at the age of 90. Nevertheless, he said, there is an obligation to do everything possible, and it is in Hashem's power to cure the Saba Kadisha. Unfortunately, these efforts were to no avail.

---

1. The righteous Dr. Wallach, founder of Shaare Zedek Hospital, revered the Saba Kadisha and attended to him faithfully, visiting him night and day, and performed many favors for him. When the Saba Kadisha was in the hospital, Dr. Wallach provided him with a spacious room and followed his wish that he be attended to only by men, not by the hospital's female nurses. He also permitted the Saba Kadisha to have visitors outside of regular visiting hours. On Shabbos, he allowed a *minyan* to convene in the Saba Kadisha's room, with a *Sefer Torah*. May Hashem bless him, and may the merit of the tzaddik stand on his behalf.

CHAPTER 15

THE THIRTEENTH DAY

THE LAST HOURS OF THE SABA KADISHA

On the morning of Tuesday, the 22nd of Iyar, a dark cloud covered our faces. We did not dream that this day would come so suddenly.

As soon as we awoke in the morning our spirits were agitated. The Rebbe instructed me to rush to the home of the Saba Kadisha to inquire as to his well-being. As the Rebbe was talking to me, messengers came running to tell us that the Saba Kadisha was still alive, but there were signs that his end was near. They asked the Rebbe to visit him before he returned his soul to his Creator.

The Rebbe's face paled and he could not answer, for he was dismayed by this news. An automobile was brought shortly thereafter, and the Rebbe removed his two pairs of tefillin. We set out immediately, with pounding hearts, and entered the house of the tzaddik.

We found him in a terrible state. His difficulty in breathing was audible, and his bed was surrounded by many pious individuals.

The Munkacser chassidim who had spent the night and morning there told the Rebbe that the Saba Kadisha and been speaking, his face radiant, the entire night, asking all those who had been with the Rebbe in Tzefas, Meron, and Teveriah about the trip. After that, he had involved himself in a halachic discussion, regarding the issue of shaving with chemicals or scissors that cut as close as a razor. Close to midnight, he instructed that *Teshuvos Minchas Eluzar* 2:48 — a lengthy explanation of the stringent views on this matter — be studied before him. He also asked that the *Zohar's* discussion of the prohibition of removing the beard be read and studied. In that way, he busied himself with halachah and Torah study until the morning.

Afterward, he was helped to don his tallis and two pairs of tefillin in bed. Usually, he wore tallis and tefillin throughout the entire davening, but this time, he wore them only during the recitation of the *Shema*. When he reached the word *"Emes"* he instructed that they be removed, saying, "Enough, enough, I can't anymore."

When the Saba Kadisha saw the Rebbe he strengthened himself, and asked him, "Why did you come now?"

"To see the face of our teacher, for he gives life to our souls," the Rebbe replied, tears rolling down his cheeks.

The Saba Kadisha accepted his words, as if to say, "Do not worry, for it will be good." He instructed him to sit, and then raised his arms from his bed and blessed him with the words, "Long life." His lips continued to move, but we could not hear what he was saying.

The Rebbe instructed the person in charge of the house to put some milk into the Saba Kadisha's holy mouth. Someone put a cup into the Saba's hand, but he refused it. The Rebbe urged him to drink a bit. He recited aloud the blessing *"Shehakol nihiyeh bidvaro."* He then drank from a spoon.

We saw that the Saba's death was near, and we were shaken and apprehensive — especially when we remembered that it is said about several tzaddikim that before their deaths they recited the *Shehakol* blessing and did not recite a concluding blessing. Their intention when saying *Shehakol* was to taste from the Tree of Life in the next world, and they had faith that at the time they would arise during the Resurrection of the Dead they would recite the concluding blessing *"Borei Nefashos,"* thanking Hashem for recreating their souls.

Of his own accord, the Saba asked that the cup of milk be brought to him, rather than the spoon they had put into his mouth previously, and he took the cup in his hand and drank. We stood there with tears in our eyes, observing that he was still alive and that one should never despair of God's mercy, as our Sages teach (*Berachos* 10a).

THE SABA KADISHA'S DEMISE

Afterwards, however — woe to the eyes that saw this — the Saba Kadisha's eyes began to roll. His lips were still moving, but his voice could no longer be heard. It seemed that he was saying something like, *"Nigmar* — it is finished." The many people and Torah scholars who filled the house began to say the verses declaring the Oneness of G-d from *Maavar Yabok,* which are customarily recited during a person's final moments.

As we recited those verses, tears pouring from our eyes, we saw the Saba Kadisha raise his right hand several times as though signaling to someone, in the manner of one who has made up his mind. He touched his hand to his holy beard, and then his soul departed immediately. (This was reminiscent of what happened with the holy Ropshitzer Rebbe, author of *Zera Kodesh.* He was in the throes of death for a long time, and his son-in-law, the holy R' Asher, said that when he would put his right hand on his beard, he would be taken to the next world. The people at the Ropshitzer's bedside began to recite the verses said when the soul departs, and then he passed away. This story was related several times by the holy author of *Darkei Teshuvah,* who also put his right hand on his beard prior to his passing.)

The Saba Kadisha died at approximately 9 a.m. He retained his faculties until the very last moment.

Woe unto us! The holy *Luchos* were broken before our eyes, the Torah was burnt in front of us!

The Rebbe threw himself prostrate onto the ground, and wailed bitterly, "Woe! The anointed one of the G-d of Yaakov!" He almost fainted, and it was with great difficulty that we managed to help him stand upright.

The Rebbe begged the Sephardic scholars in the house to depart from their custom of not immersing a deceased person in a mikveh. (The Ashkenazi and chassidic Jews in the Holy Land were accustomed to immersing many Torah scholars and tzaddikim in a mikveh, but the Sephardic Jews were not.) He asked that the Saba Kadisha should be immersed in deference to his holiness and greatness, and they agreed.

Later, however, we learned that they did not keep their word, for they wished to maintain their custom. We found out then that the main reason they did not keep their word was because they were afraid of their rabbi and leader, Yaakov Maier, a member of the official rabbinate, which the Saba Kadisha strenuously opposed. Immediately after the Saba Kadisha's demise, the zealous Torah scholars of Jerusalem warned Yaakov Maier not to come to eulogize him.

On our way out, we had to support the Rebbe on either side as we walked him to our vehicle. We went to our lodgings for Shacharis and also immersed in a mikveh in honor of the tzaddik, so that we could perhaps touch his coffin on its way to the cemetery.

The terrible news spread quickly throughout the Holy City, and it was announced in every neighborhood in the name of both the Sephardic and Ashkenazi rabbis that people should cease their work and close their stores, for the Jewish people had lost a great prince. It was also announced that the funeral would take place at 1:30 p.m. The sound of this announcement rang in our ears in the neighborhood of Kollel Munkacs. The entire city was distraught and in mourning, practically in disbelief. Who would have thought that the redemption would not have come during his lifetime? People thought that since he had lived so long, he would surely live to see the rebuilding of Jerusalem. But suddenly, he was gone, and there had hardly even been time during the few days of his final illness to pray for his recovery.

At about 2 p.m., thousands of men, women, and children, including all of the Torah leaders of Jerusalem, gathered in the Ruchamah neighborhood. When they brought the body of the Saba Kadisha out (on a wooden board, covered, not in a box or coffin as is customary in our countries), the sounds of crying did not stop, and rivers of tears flowed. The Rebbe said that there is no one in this generation worthy of eulogizing him, for no one could fathom his greatness. He, therefore, did not wish to eulogize him. Besides, he was extremely weak, moaning and wailing over the great loss. The other great men of Jerusalem followed his example and also refrained from speaking about the deceased.

In fact, no eulogies were necessary, for everyone was brokenhearted, crying and bemoaning the loss. The mourning was far greater than it would have been for a person who passed away young, leaving young orphans surrounding the coffin with no one to support them. With the Saba Kadisha's passing, everyone felt that they had lost a father, whose presence had given them life, whose merit had sustained them, and whose counsel had helped them to navigate difficult issues that arose with regard to religious matters.

The Rebbe tore his garment — in addition to the tear he had made when he saw Eretz Yisrael and the Kosel HaMaaravi for the first time — at the funeral, and walked after the *niftar* brokenheartedly among the devastated throngs. Because of the crowding, it was not possible to reach the board upon which the *niftar* lay, to carry or even touch it. It was indescribably painful to us to see the board being touched by strangers of every sort. Many of them were the kinds of people whom the Saba Kadisha fought against during his lifetime. He did not allow them to see his face, for he could not stand them. Now, they were milling about his body, and they were the ones involved in bringing him to his final resting place. Woe to the eyes that saw this! Due to the noise and the pushing of the crowd, there was nothing we could do about it. We could not even protest; may Hashem forgive us. Nevertheless, the honor of the Saba Kadisha is not diminished.

It was not physically possible to follow the coffin through the streets for the approximately three hours it would take until it arrived at Har Hazeisim. The Rebbe therefore took leave of the Saba Kadisha's body on the way, and we returned with him to our lodgings. (He also had a hidden reason for this.)

The people came back from the funeral toward evening. With the Saba Kadisha's burial we lost a human who was a repository of volumes of the revealed and hidden Torah, Tanach, Talmud Bavli and Yerushalmi, *Sifra, Sifri, Tosefta, Mechilta,* and all of the works of the *Rishonim* and *Acharonim* — along with the source of holiness and purity and the wisdom of the modern-day "Shlomo." May his merit protect us, and may we soon merit to be in his presence when

Mashiach arrives and he arises during the Resurrection of the Dead.

Remarkably, when the news spread that the Saba Kadisha had passed away, even the secularists acknowledged the manifestation of Divine Providence. It was well known that the Rebbe had wanted for a long time to travel to Jerusalem and see the Saba Kadisha. But each time he asked permission, the Saba Kadisha had turned him down, hinting in his letters that reason for the delay would later become clear. Only recently, before Pesach, he

Kever of the Saba Kadisha on Har Hazeisim

had suddenly written to the Rebbe with Divine Inspiration giving his consent for the Rebbe to come. He gave his permission in a way that made it possible for us to come to the Holy City only approximately two weeks before his demise. The Rebbe managed to meet with the Saba Kadisha several times and delight in his presence, and merited to be with him when his soul departed — the day before the Rebbe was scheduled to return home. It was obvious that Heaven had arranged it this way and that the Saba Kadisha had known with his Divine Inspiration exactly when to schedule the visit.

Later, the Rebbe visited the home of the tzaddik and chassid, Rav Baruch Feldbrand, a prominent member of our Kollel in Jerusalem. Toward evening, we went to the Kosel for Minchah. All of those

who were there were shaken when they saw how the Rebbe parted from the Kosel, kissing its stones with intense yearning, with a pained heart.

Rav Baruch Feldbrand

CHAPTER 16

PARTING FROM JERUSALEM

On Wednesday morning, the 23rd of Iyar and the fourteenth day of our stay in the Holy Land, the Jews of Jerusalem gathered to the neighborhood of Kollel Munkacs to receive the Rebbe's parting blessing. The last ship traveling from Jaffa to Trieste before Shavuos was departing today, and the Rebbe wished to return home in time for Yom Tov.

The people's hearts were heavy, and it was very difficult for them to take leave of us.

Before the Rebbe stepped onto the train platform, seeing all those who had gathered around him, thirsting for his words — especially the zealots who defend the walls of Jerusalem by fighting for Hashem's honor and His Torah — he could not contain himself. These were his final words:

> My brothers, do not fear, for despite the fire that
> Hashem brought with the felling of the wall of
> Jerusalem, the citadel, our great and awesome
> teacher, the Saba Kadisha — you and I are alike
> in the magnitude of our loss — we cannot ascribe

death to him, for his spirit and power are still with us. We will follow in his footsteps and go in the light of Hashem, helping each other, coming to the aid of Hashem against the mighty. You should not, G-d forbid, be like those who straddle both sides of the fence, flattering the evildoers. Instead, be strong! With the zeal of Hashem, stand up against the secularists and hypocrites, and institute safeguard over safeguard for our holy Torah and our holy faith, according to the tradition of our forefathers, with all its details, and without budging at all from it. Then, it will be good for you and for your children, and there will be no breach and no wailing in your streets. You should know that the eyes of all the Jews of the Diaspora are lifted to you, and yours is the task of guarding the holiness of the land. May Hashem guard the Holy City now and forever, may He be pleased with your actions, and may you be successful in everything you do to raise the banner of Torah in the holiness of purity. May we merit seeing you in joy on the holy mountain in Jerusalem, with the return of His Holy Divine Presence to Zion, and may He gather us from the four corners of the earth, speedily in our days.

With these holy words that came straight from the Rebbe's pure heart, he parted from them, crying, and they parted from him, crying, listening to his words of *mussar* with yearning. They traveled after him, escorting him until Jaffa, so that we traveled with a large entourage from Jerusalem, sorrowfully. The Holy City of Jerusalem! Fortunate is the one chosen to dwell in God's courtyard! We, however, had to distance ourselves from its holy soil, and it was exceedingly difficult to leave.

During this trip, we passed through the village of Motza where they used to pick *aravah* branches and bring them to the Beis HaMikdash (*Succah* 45a). Now, sadly, Motza is in a state of destruction, especially after the massacres of the Arabs in 5689/1929.

We also went a bit out of our way to pass through Tel Aviv. There we saw a complete city, full of beautiful buildings in the physical sense, but lowered to the depths in the spiritual sense. Many of its inhabitants desecrate Shabbos privately and publicly, eat non-kosher food, and are not careful with the laws of family purity. Unfortunately, this situation exists in other settlements as well. (One of these people admitted freely to the Rebbe that there was no mikveh in his community and the people there were not careful at all in this regard.) They have totally profaned that which is holy. May Hashem save us, and may the Owner of the vineyard come and clear away the thorns speedily in our days.

We arrived in the holy city of Jaffa between 9 and 10 a.m. We approached the port and descended into the small boat that would take us out to the ship *Carnara*, which could not come all the way to the shore because of the boulders in the water. Only small, slow-moving boats could pass through those waters, rocking back and

The Rebbe boarding the ship that would carry him back to Munkacs

forth as they moved, along with the people inside them. Many of the scholars of Jerusalem came in these boats to escort the Rebbe until the ship. There was a ladder at the side of the ship on which people would go up and down, quickly, with the help and shoving of the sailors and Arabs.

We, as well as the people escorting us, climbed up the ladder to the *Carnara*; the people of Jerusalem had come this far for they delighted in the presence of the Rebbe and basked in his wisdom. He also delighted with them, in mutual love, as they stood on the border between Eretz Yisrael and the Diaspora, until the captain's voice indicated that the ship was about to set sail. Then, our beloved companions wished us farewell and left the ship with great longing. We, too, felt tremendous longing for them.

We stood at the stern of the great ship, and as they returned on the small boat to the shore, they called out to us from the water in a bitter, wailing voice that melted our hearts: "Please remember us from afar! Keep Jerusalem in your hearts, by speaking favorably of us before the holy Rebbe, for our hearts yearn for him to shower us with spiritual life, now that we have been orphaned and we have no father in Eretz Yisrael."

As they pleaded with us from the depths of the sea, begging us to save them and channel the Rebbe's influence onto them from afar, their cries penetrated our hearts and stirred our emotions. In truth, however, it was only our bodies that were being separated. Our hearts were still close, longing for the holy city and the Beis HaMikdash, and for the *roshei yeshivos* and their students, the scholars and the tzaddikim, may Hashem's pleasantness be upon them.

CHAPTER 17

THE WAY BACK

After midday, we went to our berths. As the ship traversed the waters, we were carried steadily away from Eretz Yisrael and Jerusalem.

By this time, we were already accustomed to the sea's turbulence. On our way to Eretz Yisrael we had spent only three days on board, but now we were embarking on a trip of five consecutive days. Nevertheless, we were not as afraid of the sea, for we trusted that just as the A-mighty had brought us to Eretz Yisrael peacefully, He would return us to our destination in peace.

But while our fear of the sea was allayed, there was no way to curb our longing for Eretz Yisrael and its holy sites. Our visit seemed to have been so short, and we could hardly believe that our feet had stood in Jerusalem,[1] Tzefas, Teveriah, Meron, and the other

---

1. When the Rebbe returned to his home, he sent the following letter to the Munkacser chassidim in Jerusalem:

> Believe me, I loved the Holy Land so much, and I especially loved you, my followers who love me and are zealous for Hashem, His Torah and His faith. The thirteen days that I spent in the Holy Land correspond to the thirteen years that Rabbi Shimon bar Yochai and his son Rabbi Eluzar spent in the cave (*Shabbos* 33b), but in light of the trials of this last generation,

holy places in Eretz Yisrael for thirteen days. All members of the group had asked one another, "To where should we ascend upon our arrival in Jerusalem? And to where should we go upon our departure from Jerusalem?" This sentiment was especially intense now that the light of the world had been extinguished before our eyes with the passing of our master and teacher, the Saba Kadisha, whom we can never forget.

The Rebbe was inconsolable, as well. The entire way, he mourned bitterly for the Saba Kadisha, like a son confessing before his Father in Heaven, saying: "I was full when I went away, but I have been brought back empty." Immediately, however, he strengthened himself and his spirit returned. As tears poured from his eyes he said, "The tzaddik, the Saba Kadisha, can still accomplish in the heavens. The Redeemer will rush to redeem those broken by this bitter exile, for tzaddikim are greater in their deaths than in their lives, and David, the king of Israel, lives and endures."

While relating this incident, I am reminded of what transpired on Motza'ei Shabbos, the night of 23 Iyar, when the Rebbe went to the upper deck to breathe some fresh sea air. (He had not gone outdoors onto the ship's deck all of Friday night or Shabbos day.) We, the members of his group, were surrounding him, and he spoke about the Saba Kadisha's holiness with tears on his face. "The Saba Kadisha is certainly now in the the Sanctuary of Mashiach, relating there what happened to him in this world and telling about the people he was close to during his life, who are now mourning for him like orphans. He will certainly arouse mercy on them, on us, and on all of the Jewish people, interceding favorably for them and binding up their sorrows with their speedy salvation. May the Merciful One send us his Mashiach speedily in our days."

---

may Hashem in His goodness consider one day in place of each year, but this is not the place to explain at length. Those days are engraved upon my memory until and beyond the arrival of the Redeemer, speedily in our days. At night, as well, my heart does not sleep from awe of holiness. It is as though I were lying in a shul, inside an *aron kodesh*. I will therefore delineate to you several matters that should be before you and inside your hearts so that you should know to watch and be exceedingly careful...

Members of the entourage aboard the ship

This and other matters made our voyage on this ship less than joyous. On our voyage to Eretz Yisrael, the only Jews on the ship had been the members of our group. The Satan had not shown himself, and there were no alien Jews among us. This was not the case upon our return from Eretz Yisrael, however. On this voyage, the ship was full of young men and women who made a mockery of Judaism. When they spoke, in their made-up Hebrew language, it was as though they were stabbing us with swords, for this modern corruption of the Holy Tongue for mundane use is surely hated by Hashem and loathsome in the eyes of all Jews in whom the fire of Torah still burns. Thank God, we did not have any interaction with these people, but occasionally we saw and heard their comings and goings.

I must relate what my own eyes saw of the actions of these people. On Shabbos, I went up on the deck with a member of our group, the renowned chassid R' Chaim Baruch Ehrenberg of Strask. As we passed the large hall, we saw a woman, who spoke only Hebrew to her children, sitting and writing a letter, in full view! When we told her that today is the holy Shabbos, she simply ignored us.

The Rebbe learning on the ship

Among the Jewish passengers on the ship were also a number that belonged to the Agudah. On Shabbos morning, these Jews asked the Rebbe to give them his *Sefer Torah* (which he had brought along with him on the trip) to read from in their early morning *minyan*. The Rebbe responded that no Shabbos desecrator had ever been called up to or made a blessing on this *Sefer Torah*,[2] which he had inherited from his holy father. If they could guarantee, he said, that no Shabbos desecrators or sinners would be called to the Torah in their *minyan*, he would grant them permission to read from his *Sefer Torah*. But they could not provide this guarantee.

Except for these disturbances, our voyage was uneventful. Even on Shabbos, which was already the fourth day of our trip, we did not lack delicacies. We still had fruits, challos, and aged fine wine from the Holy Land, which we had been given for the trip. We

---

2. The Rebbe wrote in *Minchas Eluzar* 5:52 (a handwritten manuscript that was unfortunately lost) that a Shabbos desecrator should absolutely not be called up to the Torah, and should certainly not be one of the seven people called up for *aliyos*.

also had delicious fish that the owners of the ship had given us on Friday. The fish was fresh and we were able to cook it. With all these foods, our Shabbos table was set with much abundance, and we delighted in the holy Shabbos. We especially enjoyed the spiritual sustenance that the Rebbe provided us, with his holy words, Torah discussions, and prayers.

Hashem was with us during our trip, and with His help we arrived at the port of Trieste on Monday morning.

We had barely left the ship, and our legs were still wobbly from the voyage, when we heard that the newspapers in these lands had spread terrible rumors and lies during our stay in Eretz Yisrael, reporting that the Rebbe had fallen ill. Munkacser chassidim throughout Europe had been gripped with fear, and the city of Munkacs was especially shaken, even though they had received telegrams from us with good reports. They had even arranged for local government officials to inquire through the Czechoslovakian Consulate in Jerusalem as to the Rebbe's well-being, and had been told that he was healthy and well. (When the Rebbe arrived in Jerusalem, the consul sent a delegation to welcome him warmly, and he also notified the Rebbe that he wished to visit him at his lodgings. However, in deference to the honor of the government of our country, the Rebbe went to visit the consul in his residence. The consul was delighted to meet him, and because of this meeting he was able to assure the people of Munkacs that the Rebbe was well. But we knew nothing of this exchange.) When they had received the positive report from the consul, the enemies' faces had darkened, and the Jews had rejoiced. Nevertheless, due to the great distance between us, they were not entirely certain that the Rebbe was well, but they had faith in Hashem that surely no tragedy had befallen us.

Later, it became clear who had been responsible for the libelous reports. When they heard of the great honor accorded to the Rebbe in the Holy Land, and how Munkacser chassidim everywhere were rejoicing, they channeled their fury into a libelous report to frighten the people in this cruel manner. They had no qualms about spreading these lies even though the truth was bound to be revealed. At the end, they were shamed.

While we were in Trieste, Munkacser chassidim and members of the Munkacser yeshivah asked me to try to convince the Rebbe to arrange his trip in such a way that we would arrive back in Munkacs during the day, not at night. They were preparing a festive reception with soldiers in full array, and with music and dancing upon his safe return, and it would be a greater honor if he were to return during the day.

The Rebbe insisted on arriving at night, however, for he understood that the chassidim were making many preparations for his arrival, and he wished to flee from honor. Besides, we were distraught over the loss of the Saba Kadisha. News of his passing had not yet reached these lands, and all along our train voyage from Trieste to Vienna to Munkacs, the chassidim who had come to greet the Rebbe had inquired as to the welfare of the Saba Kadisha. Neither the Rebbe nor we wished to relate the bad news. The Rebbe therefore preferred that he be inconspicuous upon his arrival.

We came home in the wee hours of the morning of the second day of Sivan. Despite the hour, men, women, and children came out to greet the Rebbe, and the city of Munkacs rejoiced. Candles were lit in the windows of the houses, and bright lights and flags were places on the large gate in the middle of the city. (The Rebbe did not wish to travel through that gate, however, and he took a different route instead.) How beautiful was the scene of the reception of the great king!

But the Rebbe cautioned the people not to play music, for the heart knows its own bitterness (*Mishlei* 14:10).[3] The *shivah* for the

---

3. The following is from *Toldos Rabbeinu* (170):

> Open your eyes and see in *Mass'os Yerushalayim* the time that the Rebbe returned from Eretz Yisrael to his holy abode. It was in the wee hours of the morning of 2 Sivan, 5690 (1930), and he did not allow the people coming to welcome him from this great and holy journey with singing and music.
>
> This was remarkable, for at almost that exact time, during the early morning of 2 Sivan 5697 (1937), the Rebbe's pure soul departed to the Heavens, and darkness covered the earth. The Rebbe lived exactly seven years after his trip to Eretz Yisrael. During that time, the entire world was sustained in the physical sense and in the spiritual sense. May we yet live to see the king in his splendor with the Resurrection of the Dead.

Saba Kadisha was almost finished, but we were still in the thirty days of mourning for the loss of the tzaddik; how could we sing?

It was with great ceremony that we reached the royal courtyard of the Rebbe's house, accompanied by the Jews who had gathered to greet him upon his return from his momentous journey. When the Rebbe arrived at his home, it was already dawn. The people were calling out, "Long live our Master, our Teacher, our Rebbe." May he guide and carry us forever, and lead us toward Mashiach, speedily in our days.

With the passing of the tzaddik, the shield of the generation, we saw the fulfillment of the verse (*Yeshayah* 57:1), "Because of the impending evil the righteous one was gathered in." Shortly after the Rebbe's passing, the Nazis began to persecute the Jews of the neighboring lands, eventually subjecting men, women, and children, including many great Torah leaders, to the cruelest of deaths.

In Adar 5704/1944, the enemy cast his net over Hungary, and in Nissan the Jews of Munkacs were sent to the ghetto. On the 20th of Iyar, the Nazis began to transport people daily from the Munkacs region to Auschwitz, the valley of death. The final transport was loaded onto the cattle-cars on the afternoon of the first day of Sivan, and the people on the transport stayed in the cattle-cars overnight at the brick factory near the cemetery. On 2 Sivan, they traveled to Auschwitz. At that horrific time, our brothers recalled how exactly seven years earlier on that day, the Rebbe had passed away. And seven years before that, on that very day, the Rebbe had said, "The heart knows its own bitterness." He had seen in his crystal-clear vision what would eventually happen on this day. We, however, did not know what was to befall us until we experienced these horrors ourselves. We lost parents and children, and were left few in number, with no one to turn to but our Father in Heaven.

O Gracious One, look down from on high! See how the blood of the righteous has been spilled, and remove the stains, O King Who sits on the Throne of Mercy!

THE LIFE AND TEACHINGS
OF THE "SABA KADISHA"

Rabbi Shlomo Eliezer Elfandri

His Lineage

Rabbi Shlomo Eliezer Elfandri was born around the year 5570-5575 (1810-1815) to his father R' Yaakov and his mother Chana, in the Turkish capital, previously known as Constantinople or Costadina, and currently known as Istanbul. His exact date of birth is not known, but he said about himself that in the year 5600 (1840) he was at the forefront of the battle to save the Jews of Damascus from a blood libel (see Chapter 8). We can assume that if he was acting as a leader in the capital city of Damascus, he was probably about 30 at the time. (It was also known in Jerusalem that a certain tzaddik was younger than the Saba Kadisha. This calculation concurs with that information.)

His father was a Torah scholar, but he did not live very long. His mother lived into her 80's, however. She was an erudite woman, and she taught her son privately during his childhood.

On his father's side, he was descended from the great sages, R' Chaim Elfandri (whose greatness is described in the Chida's *Shem HaGedolim*) and his son R' Yaakov, author of *Teshuvos Mutzal MeiEish*. His family was from the tribe of Judah, tracing its distinguished lineage back to King David and Betzalel.

On his mother's side, he was from the family of the author of *Nachalah L'Yehoshua* (who lived during the lifetime of the Beis Yosef), who was the grandfather of the author of *Knesses HaGedolah*. (See *Shem HaGedolim* in the section on R' Yehoshua Zunzin. The Zunzin family was a distinguished one, as described in *Shem HaGedolim*, ibid. and Introduction.)

The Saba Kadisha related the following story about his lineage:

There was a certain distinguished woman who married a rav and had a son whose name was R' Chaim Abulafia. When her husband died, she remarried and had another son whose name was R' Chaim Elgazi. (Sephardic Jews are not stringent about giving the same name to two brothers, or to a father and a son.) The second husband died, and she traveled to Istanbul, where she married a third time and had a son who was known as R' Chaim Elfandri, the Elder. (This was the Saba Kadisha's grandfather.) These three brothers grew up, and each one became a rav in a different city. They were all renowned Torah leaders, but they did not see each other or know each other.

The three brothers always longed to meet one another. But in those days, travel was very difficult, especially by sea. Once, however, it happened that they all had to travel by ship to different destinations. While they were traveling, a storm hit, and Hashem arranged it that all three of their ships docked at the same port on an island and they were miraculously saved.

Because the brothers were each outstanding individuals, and it was evident on their faces that they were distinguished people, they discovered that were brothers, and they lovingly kissed each other. (The story does not end there. The three brothers boarded a ship together, and once again, the ship was in danger of capsizing. The brothers were immersed in Torah discussion, and when they became aware of the danger, the two older ones stood up to pray, but they were not answered until the third, youngest brother — R' Chaim Elfandri — stood up to pray. As soon as he began praying, the storm abated.)

The Saba Kadisha also related that R' Naftali Katz, author of *Semichus Chachamim*, came to Istanbul, intending to continue on to Eretz Yisrael. The Saba Kadisha's grandfather (either R' Chaim or R' Yaakov) recognized him, and advised him to settle in Istanbul. R' Naftali followed this advice, and he built a large shul in Istanbul that carries his name, which stands until this very day. Later, when R' Naftali had trouble with some enemies, the Saba Kadisha's grandfather sent him an inkwell and a quill in a golden box, along with a large golden sword, telling him that with this sword he should stand up against his enemies. From then on, anyone who spoke against R' Naftali in the slightest immediately collapsed and never again got up. When the people heard of this, they became afraid, and he was able to live in peace. (Later, that sword was given to the king, and he succeeded in the wars he was fighting then.)

R' Chaim Elfandri had a large yeshivah in Istanbul, with many great students, among them sixty brilliant, holy rabbanim who were a great source of pride to him. He referred to them as "the sixty mighty ones." During his time, the great R' Yitzchak of Trani served as a rav in Istanbul, and he said that he envies R' Chaim for his sixty students. Each of these students knew one entire tractate of Talmud by heart, so that during learning they did not need to waste time looking things up, for they themselves were the Talmud.

One Erev Pesach, when R' Chaim was old, he sent a special messenger to each of these sixty students secretly, without the knowledge of the others. He instructed them to come to him that day toward evening, about half an hour before nightfall.

The city of Istanbul is divided into many different districts, each surrounded by water. To go from one district to another, it is necessary to travel by boat. R' Chaim lived at the edge of the districts, and the students therefore understood that it would not be possible for them to return home for the Seder. Nevertheless, they all came. They brought their own matzos, wine, and other necessities for the Seder and the first days of Pesach. When they all arrived at the home of their teacher, who was still completely healthy, they wondered why they had been summoned, but they did not dare to ask.

R' Chaim davened Minchah and Maariv with them and conducted the Seder together with them. When the Seder was over, he called each one of them over and blessed him. After that he told them, "My dear students, declare the greatness of Hashem with me, and let us exalt His Name together for the last time. Say *Shema Yisrael* with me, and prepare yourselves now for this."

With a loud, mighty voice they said the verse of *Shema Yisrael* together with their rebbi, and his soul departed as they said the word "*Echad.*" They then understood why they had been summoned.

The Saba Kadisha related that when he was a child of around 6 or 7, his impoverished parents were living in a house that the community had provided for them. It had originally been built for a certain great rav who wanted to live near the mikveh, so that he could immerse himself whenever he wished. The house had a door that opened to the mikveh, and there were three or four rooms in the living quarters. His maternal grandmother, a member of the Zunzin family, lived with them, in her own room.

Every night, they heard derisive, abusive voices coming from the mikveh. When they opened the door to investigate, they did not see anyone, and they understood that the voices were coming from evil spirits and demons. This went on for several nights, and they suffered greatly from it.

When they apprised the leader of the community of what was going on, he told them, "From the time that the rav who lived in this house passed away, this house was given to several poor people, and they were all forced to leave. Apparently, the rav disapproved of the people living in his house, but I thought that because you were from such a distinguished family, the spirits would be afraid of you and your holy ancestors."

When they heard this, the old woman told her grandson, "Shlomo Eliezer, gather the keys to all the rooms of the house. Throw them into the mikveh, and say, 'If you insist on living here, here are the keys. We will leave the house, since we and you cannot live together under one roof.'"

"My dear grandmother," he answered her, "I will not give them the keys, but I will go and tell them, 'We are paupers and we do not have anywhere else to live. The community gave us the keys to live here, and we are therefore the owners of the house and you should leave the mikveh, for you have no right to stay here.'"

When the old woman heard this, she laughed and was pleased. "Good, good," she told him. "That is what you should say, if you wish."

And that is what happened. The child went to the mikveh and spoke, and from then on, no more voices were heard.

When the Saba Kadisha was 17 or 18, he got married and had a son. But Hashem took this child when he was still young, and the Saba Kadisha never had children after that. His wife died when he was already an old man, and he did not remarry.

ISTANBUL

The Saba Kadisha was born and raised in Istanbul, and it appears that he lived there most of his life. He taught Torah there for many years, not budging from the beis medrash. That was where he earned his glorious reputation, which spread throughout the cities of Turkey. In Istanbul, especially, the people flocked to hear Torah from his mouth.

Wealthy people, wise people, and rabbanim sought to learn with him, but he drew near to himself only those who found favor in his eyes. He would choose people whose fear of God took priority over their wisdom. Most of his close students were great rabbanim who were older than he, and understood the depths of his Torah learning. He learned Torah with them most of the day.

By the time he was about 30, he was chosen to be part of the local council for spiritual matters. At that time, he had forty disciples, all of whom were older than he. These disciples became great rabbanim, outstanding in their Torah knowledge and ability to rule in halachic matters. (The author of *Sdei Chemed* was one of the disciples who studied in the Saba Kadisha's yeshivah in Istanbul.)

As mentioned earlier, the city of Istanbul was divided into a number of districts, each of which contained a large Jewish populace and had its own rav. In the Saba Kadisha's district, the people pleaded with him to become the rav. They appointed him to this post and gave him the title of rav. The Saba Kadisha, however, did not wish to derive benefit from the crown of Torah and refused to accept a salary. When they called him the rav of the city he said, "I am not a rav." He also did not wear the rabbinic turban like most of the Sephardim, choosing instead to dress like one of the simple people. Nevertheless, when asked to rule on halachic matters, he answered anyone who came to seek the word of Hashem. In interpersonal matters, he refrained from adjudicating as much as possible, but when people pressed him to, he agreed. After hearing the arguments of both sides, he would answer briefly, "This one says this and this one says that, you are guilty and you are innocent" — and no more. The plaintiffs would accept his judgment without a word, for they were in awe of him, knowing that those who defied him would be punished.

The scholars and rabbanim of the city exhorted the Saba Kadisha to join the central *beis din*, but he refused, for he wished to devote himself to Torah study. Nevertheless, people from all of the districts and yeshivos of Istanbul brought the most difficult matters to him.

Among the greatest of his disciples was the renowned R' Yitzchak Akrish, author of *Kiryas Arba*. R' Yitzchak was an elderly scholar and a great zealot, who constantly sanctified Hashem's Name at great personal risk. Several times, he was imprisoned because of his firm stand on religious matters, and his rebbi, the Saba Kadisha, came to his aid and rescued him each time. He was also very poor, and he had a family to support.

Once, R' Yitzchak asked his rebbi to try to help him find a post as the rav of one of the districts of Istanbul, so that he could support his family honorably. The Saba Kadisha answered him, "I will try to help you find a position as a rav, but only on condition that you promise that whichever district of Istanbul accepts you as rav, you will not turn down the position."

After R' Yitzchak gave his word, the Saba Kadisha tried to have him be accepted as the rav in the district where he himself lived. R' Yitzchak did not wish to be the rav in his rebbi's district, but he had already promised to accept any post in Istanbul that the Saba Kadisha would arrange for him.

The people of the district considered it a disgrace to appoint a rav in the Saba Kadisha's stead, even though R' Yitzchak was a renowned and respected individual. But from that time, the Saba Kadisha did not wish to rule in any halachic matters. He rented a house in his neighborhood for R' Yitzchak, and whenever people approached him with questions he would send them to him, saying, "That is where the rav lives." The people therefore had no choice but to accept R' Yitzchak as their rav and to give him a respectable salary.

On his first Shabbos as rav, R' Yitzchak gave a public address, and all of the Torah scholars, rabbanim, and community leaders of Istanbul came to hear it. After he finished his address, the Saba Kadisha spoke, expounding the verse (*Bamidbar* 27:16), "May Hashem, G-d of the spirits of all flesh, appoint a man over the assembly, who shall go out before them and come in before them, who shall take them out and bring them in; and let the assembly of Hashem not be like sheep that have no shepherd." The Saba Kadisha pointed out several difficulties with this verse:

1. It should have said, "appoint a man *for* the assembly," not "*over* the assembly."
2. If the verse states that the person will "go out before them," it did not have to say that he will also "come in before them." Furthermore, the repetition of the phrase "before them" seems redundant.
3. Similarly, it did not have to say both that the person will "take them out" and that he will "bring them in."
4. It should have said, "and let the assembly of Hashem not be without a shepherd," rather than, "and let the assembly of Hashem not be like sheep that have no shepherd."

The Saba Kadisha addressed these difficulties by explaining that nowadays, unfortunately, a rav is appointed only for the purpose of ruling what is forbidden and what is permitted. With regard to other issues in the city, no one is interested in what he has to say. Instead, they follow the opinion of the laypeople. Furthermore, they misquote him, saying that the rav instructed such-and-such when he never said anything of the sort, and the rav does not protest. It therefore becomes unclear who is in charge: Does the rav control the people, or do they control him?

That is why, when describing what a leader should be, Moshe said — in repetitive language, for emphasis — that Hashem should appoint a man *over* the assembly. He should be leader over them, not they over him. The leader has to "go in" and "come out" *before* the people — he should not be dragged after their opinions; rather, they should follow his. "And let the assembly of Hashem not be like sheep that have no shepherd" — this seemingly awkward phraseology connotes a situation where the people do indeed have a leader, but appear to have no leader because it is unclear who is leading whom. "The most important thing," said the Saba Kadisha, "is that the leader should not flatter anyone, and he should rule over everyone in the city through the Torah he teaches them."

R' Yitzchak Akrish was the rav for several years, but then insolent people arose and he was unable to stand up to them. He went to the holy city of Chevron, and the Saba Kadisha helped him with the expenses of the trip and helped to support him there for the rest of his life.

It is reasonable to assume that during the time that R' Yitzchak was rav, the Saba Kadisha was a decisive influence in the community's spiritual matters, fighting valiantly for religious issues just as he did before and after R' Yitzchak's stint as rav.

Once, the Saba Kadisha found out that a certain merchant had imported a large shipment of wine. The supervision had not been as he had stipulated, so he prohibited the wine. This merchant was a relative of a prominent local rav, and he was also a scholar and a community leader. He and his relative, the rav, wanted to permit the wine, especially considering the great loss that he would suffer otherwise. But they could not go against the Saba Kadisha, for his word was decisive.

Year after year, many scholars would complain about the wheat for Pesach that was brought to Istanbul from afar. Finally, the Saba Kadisha took ten of his best students and traveled on horseback for three days in the desert until they reached the place where the wheat was grown and sold. Those guarding the wheat were simple people, and the Saba Kadisha did not approve of their supervision, because there was abundant rainfall in that area, which could cause the wheat to become *chametz* unless it was protected. The supervisors pressured him to be lenient, and the gentiles, who were murderous, violent people, pressured him as well. They practically wanted to kill him, but he escaped miraculously. The Saba Kadisha and his students did not know the way back, but Hashem helped them to return to Istanbul in just one day.

After that, he arranged for God-fearing people and scholars to travel with the merchants responsible for guarding the wheat. Their salary was to be paid by the community, and they had to swear that they would not accept even a penny from the merchants. He instituted other safeguards in this matter, as well, and all of his instructions were followed.

Similarly, the Saba Kadisha took swift action when he learned that the halachic safeguards instituted by R' Yitzchak of Trani and written in the community's ledger were not being adhered to. He approached the rabbanim and community leaders to attend to this matter, but they did not obey. When he saw this, he arranged for a large amount of meat to be secretly slaughtered at night, enough for the entire city. In the morning, he posted signs and instructed that it be announced in his name that none of the meat in the city is kosher, and that whoever wants to eat meat that he certifies as kosher can find it in a certain place.

He did this for three days in a row. When the butchers saw that no one was buying their meat, they tried to get the other rabbanim in the city to forbid the meat that was under the Saba Kadisha's supervision. They, however, did not wish to do this. They said that they could not stand up against a person of the Saba Kadisha's stature, for they feared him and his Torah. The rabbanim, the slaughterers, the inspectors, the community leaders, and the butchers agreed to accept upon themselves and their children to adhere to the safeguards of R' Yitzchak of Trani. They signed a document that the Saba Kadisha prepared, and announcements went out immediately that the old slaughter was kosher once again.

It happened once that the Saba Kadisha disputed the validity of a marriage ceremony that took place in his neighborhood, and he did not permit the couple to be alone together. The matter came before the central *beis din*, which looked into the halachah and validated the marriage. When they learned that the Saba Kadisha disagreed, however, they retracted their opinion in deference to his, and they performed another marriage ceremony and *Sheva Berachos*. Although there was an ancient directive from R' Yitzchak of Trani that the decisions of the central *beis din* were not to be disputed, they nevertheless bowed to the Saba Kadisha's opinion, on the grounds that he was different, because his Torah learning was so extraordinary.

When the great R' Chaim Palagi came to Istanbul, all the rabbanim and *batei din* went to greet him, but the Saba Kadisha went alone to meet with him privately. R' Chaim asked if he had seen his pamphlet about the stringency of the commandment of Shabbos. The Saba Kadisha answered, "I saw it, but there is nothing new in it, for the Torah states explicitly (*Shemos* 31:14), 'Its desecrators shall be put to death.'"

When he left, the rabbanim said that his name befits him, for his initials — *shin, aleph* — spell *aish*, fire.

The great R' Raphael David HaLevi of Istanbul (from whom a lengthy responsum is printed in *Shemen HaMishchah* on the Rambam) once came to visit and noticed a ruling of the Saba Kadisha on the table. R' Raphael David read it. When the wife of the Saba Kadisha passed by, R' Raphael David told her, "Your husband is a wealthy man." She asked him what wealth he was referring to and he said, "He does not write in his letters, 'according to the paucity of my opinion' [i.e., in my humble opinion], so he must be wealthy in knowledge."

One Friday night, when the great R' Raphael Yitzchak Yisrael, rav of Rudis and later *Raavad* of Jerusalem,[1] was visiting Istanbul, the Saba Kadisha saw through his window that the rav was going to eat the Shabbos meal at the home of a certain person. The Saba

---

1. R' Raphael Yitzchak Yisrael is mentioned in the works of R' Chaim Palagi and in the works *Pesach HaDevir* and *Teshuvos MiPi Aharon*. His prolific writings and Torah novellae remained in the hands of his grandson, the rav of the Sephardic Jews of Chevron, who was murdered in the riots of 1929. All of the manuscripts were burned.

Kadisha did not approve of his eating there, and he motioned to him to come inside. He sent for wine and food to be brought in the rav's honor, and they began discussing Torah. The two delved deeply into halachic matters all night long, until their students came and told them that it was time to recite the morning *Shema*.

The rav of Rudis said about the Saba Kadisha that he was proficient in all areas of Torah.

Once, in Istanbul, at a gathering attended by several secular Jews, he overheard them arguing about why earthquakes occur. The Saba Kadisha stood up and said, "Know, that even if your reasons and investigations would show that it is impossible for there to be an earthquake now, if Hashem wants there to be one, it will happen supernaturally." As he spoke, there was an earthquake throughout Istanbul. Fear of God fell on everyone, and the Saba Kadisha became known as a miracle worker.

Once, a well-known rav and scholar from Jerusalem came to Istanbul. He visited the Saba Kadisha's home to consult with him and to request his help in obtaining a sizeable inheritance that had been left for his kollel by a certain wealthy man. The Saba Kadisha accorded him great honor in front of the elders and leaders of the city so that he would be able to obtain the bequest from the heirs in a dignified way. He went to hear this rav's lecture, and he himself lectured about the mitzvah to fulfill the instructions of the deceased and inspired the people to help the rav carry out his mission successfully.

When the rav would go into the Saba Kadisha's yeshivah to hear what was being studied, he would argue with what the Saba Kadisha was teaching. To this, the Saba Kadisha would answer respectfully, in his great humility. Everyone was perplexed by this, and they concluded that this rav must be a great man if the Saba Kadisha answers him so submissively.

Before this scholar took leave of the Saba Kadisha and Istanbul (after he managed to obtain the inheritance), the Saba Kadisha called him to his home privately and told him, "You should know that I accorded you honor for the sake of the poor Torah scholars in Jerusalem whom you are representing. With regard to the difficulties you posed to me during the *shiurim*, I answered you in a way that would not embarrass you in front of the scholars and would allow you to achieve your desired goal. Now, however, you will see that all the questions you raised were not difficult at all, because you did not fully understand me."

The Saba Kadisha went on to show the rav how his questions and objections were flawed. The rav readily conceded, and thanked the Saba Kadisha for not embarrassing him publicly and for showing him the truth. He fell to the Saba Kadisha's feet and kissed them, saying, "Fortunate is the generation in which the rav lives, and fortunate is the city Istanbul that produced this giant." He bent his head to be blessed, and they parted in peace.

The custom in the Sephardic countries was that wealthy people would make a large *seudah* on the yahrtzeit of their father. They would invite the scholars in their city to their homes to learn Mishnayos and distribute money generously to them. The Saba Kadisha, however, would not go to the home of any wealthy person — unless he needed his assistance to rectify some religious matter. Then, he would go of his own accord to the wealthy man's house. This only increased people's respect for him and his words, and it was considered a great merit when he would come to a person's home. It was said that when the Saba Kadisha came to someone's home, that person would see a marked increase in his business success for an entire year.

Once, the Saba Kadisha's students asked him, "Why does our master the Rav embarrass us by wearing plain clothing, like a simple person?"

He replied, "Know, my children, that I could go around in royal apparel of turquoise and white and a large gold crown, but I am concerned for you and your honor. If I were to spend money on expensive clothing, it would be, thank God, all from my own and not from others, for I have the money. But if you would then want to do as I do and wear honorable rabbinic garments, you might not have money to do so, and you will have to then go and curry favor with the wealthy people in the city to get them to give you money. If you do that, you will be unable to rebuke them in matters of Heaven, and this will bring destruction to the city. I therefore wear simple clothing for your sake, so that you, too, will suffice with this minimum. This is a safeguard for the laws of our holy Torah."

In one of his lectures for the purpose of strengthening the settlement of Torah scholars in Eretz Yisrael, he explained the juxtaposition of the ideas in the verse (*Devarim* 8:9), "A Land where you will eat bread without poverty — you will lack nothing there; a Land whose stones are iron and from whose mountains you will mine copper."

"Torah scholars are called 'stones,'" he said (see *Bava Basra* 145b). "When is it a land whose stones are iron — i.e., that the Torah scholars in it are strong as iron, bending their will to that of the Torah and not listening to or fearing evildoers and heretics? Only when it is a land in which 'you will eat bread without poverty.' When those who seek God do not lack for livelihood, then they have the ability to stand up to defend the Torah and not flatter anyone. It is therefore incumbent on us to support Torah scholars in any way we can" (quoted in *Shulchan HaMaarachah* of R' Moshe Aharon Tonkelong, one of the leaders of the Council of Supporters of Traditional Education).

A TURNING POINT

When he was still living in Istanbul, representatives of the people of Damascus urged him to become their rav. He refused to accept the position, however, explaining that if he does not conduct himself with the trappings of the rabbinate in his hometown of Istanbul it is inconsequential, but if he were to come to a new city, in the capacity of an official rav, he would be required to wear rabbinical garb. He considered this to be burdensome, and he therefore rejected the offer.

Providence ordained, however, that he should move to Damascus. Once, a wealthy, learned and generous person passed away. During his lifetime, he held a high-ranking position in the government, and was one of the city's leaders. But he had frequently curried favor and sided with the secularists.

Before the day when the community representatives met to decide religious matters, the Saba Kadisha would go early to this man's home and instruct him clearly on how to proceed without abetting the evildoers. On several occasions, the Saba Kadisha accomplished important things through this person.

Once, the government decided to draft Jews into the army. Despite the Saba Kadisha's tireless efforts to ensure that this decree would not be passed and that Jewish souls would not be endangered, his efforts were to no avail. Many influential Jews were in favor of the decree.

On the day the matter was to be decided conclusively, the Saba Kadisha went to the home of this wealthy, powerful person to beg him to intercede. He spoke to him for about three hours, but the man insisted that it was necessary to agree that Jews be drafted to the army. The Saba Kadisha warned him that his end would be bitter, but to no avail.

That afternoon, the man went to the meeting, and the decree was passed into law. On the spot, the man fainted and died.

The following day, the entire Jewish community came to the funeral to pay their final respects, for this man was very influential and had done many favors for his people. Government officials came to the funeral as well.

The custom in Istanbul was that no one would eulogize a person until the rav of the city did so, and the Saba Kadisha was the rav of that district. When the coffin was brought out, it was announced that the rav should come to deliver his eulogy. But the rav did not come. Finally the assemblage realized that he was not there. Messengers were sent to the Saba Kadisha's home, but he refused to come. Other, more distinguished people then came to him, but he still refused to attend. Finally, all of the scholars and rabbanim of Istanbul came to ask him to come, or to at least to give permission to others to eulogize the deceased.

The Saba Kadisha was intractable, however. He answered that he would not go to the funeral, and he would not give permission to others to deliver eulogies. "He is not deserving of honor," the Saba Kadisha said.

The rabbanim left and told the sons of the deceased what the Saba Kadisha had said. The coffin had been outside for several hours already, and the children of the deceased were mortified.

Rabbi Shlomo Eliezer Elfandri / 209

Accompanied by the government officials, they went to the Saba Kadisha. One of the sons put before the Saba Kadisha a purse full of gold dinars and asked him to come and honor their late father. He added that he was donating this money for the rav to distribute to tzedakah in his father's merit. The government officials also beseeched the Saba Kadisha not to humiliate the deceased and his children.

The Saba Kadisha stood up, and with tears on his face he said, "As a servant of the King of kings, the Holy One, Blessed is He, I was at the home of this man yesterday, begging him to defend our community. He refused to listen. He destroyed the city and the country by agreeing to the idea of the evildoers. Therefore, now that he was punished and died, this is what should be done to him, and no amount of pleading will help you. I do not want money and I will not eulogize the deceased." He returned the money to them, and they left his house, distraught. Needless to say, there were no eulogies.

This incident caused a great uproar in the city. The people who were faithful to Hashem understood an inkling of the greatness of the giant residing among them, who feared no one and would not tolerate flatterers.

After this incident, the Saba Kadisha said that he did not wish to reside in a city whose leaders were evildoers (even though they were all punished subsequently by Heaven), and he agreed to become the rav of Damascus.

There was another episode in Istanbul when he displayed great personal sacrifice in the matter of Jews serving in the army. There was certain *Chacham Bashi* [Chief Rabbi], Moshe Levi, who had a document in his possession from the times of the earlier kings stating that the Jews should not serve in the army. One day, King Abd El Hamud sent for the *Chacham Bashi*. The viceroy was there, and he told the *Chacham Bashi*, "Know that the king is a friend of the Jews and he wants them to serve in the army, and you therefore have to return your document to the king."

The king was known to be ruthless when someone disobeyed him. He would put that person and his family into sacks and throw them into the sea. He would do this even to his royal officers. It is understandable, therefore, that the Jews were afraid of him.

The *Chacham Bashi* gathered all the Jewish leaders to decide what to do. He did not call the Saba Kadisha, however, for he reasoned that the Saba Kadisha was a zealot who will have no fear of the king, and will be opposed to Jews serving in the army.

The Saba Kadisha heard about this matter, and he cried a loud and bitter cry that reached the royal palace. Nothing happened to him, however. Not only did Hashem save him from the lion's mouth, but the king actually helped him and appointed him to be the *Chacham Bashi* in Damascus and ruled that all of his instructions should be upheld.

DAMASCUS

At that time, the great R' Yitzchak Abulafia, author of *Teshuvos Pnei Yitzchak*, was a rav in Damascus. When the Saba Kadisha was told that the *Pnei Yitzchak* did not allow any other rav to live in Damascus, he decided not to go there, even though he had authorization from all of the scholars and wealthy leaders of the city to rule in religious matters, and despite the government ruling that everything the Saba Kadisha decreed must be obeyed.

When R' Yitzchak Abulafia heard that the Saba Kadisha was considering moving to Damascus, he sent a secret messenger, a rav from the city of Andrinea near Istanbul, to convince him not to come. The messenger spoke to the Saba Kadisha's wife, asking her to convince her husband not to travel to Damascus. "Your husband will not have peace there because of R' Abulafia, who quashes the rulings of other rabbanim with his Torah," he explained, adding that a number of Torah giants had already fled Damascus, having been considered insignificant in comparison with R' Yitzchak.

The Saba Kadisha's wife told her husband, "My master, my husband! Here, you are a renowned Torah giant. All your words are respected like the words of Moshe from G-d's mouth, and the other scholars of the city are in awe of your Torah. But there, in

Damascus, Chacham Abulafia will refute all of your Torah learning and eclipse you in halachah, so why you should move there?"

The Saba Kadisha answered, "Until now I was unsure whether to go to Damascus, but now that I heard that Chacham Abulafia is so great in Torah, I have decided to go. Here, there is no one from whom I can learn Torah. There, he will be my teacher, and I will be his student."

The Saba Kadisha traveled to Damascus and was welcomed there with great honor.

When he arrived in Damascus, he and R' Yitzhak Abulafia spent several days together involved in complex Torah discussions. The Saba Kadisha said that not once was he vanquished by the *Pnei Yitzchak*, even though the latter was a giant in Torah and halachah. The *Pnei Yitzchak* said about the Saba Kadisha that his learning was like that of the *Rishonim*. He wrote the following about him (*Teshuvos MiPi Aharon* 4:113): "Who can come after King Solomon! Hashem is with him — i.e., the halachah follows his opinion, fortunate is the woman who gave birth to him, there is no calculating his understanding." (See ibid., *Even HaEzer* 22, for a lengthy responsa from the Saba Kadisha regarding the Karaites. See also the conclusion of the author of *MiPi Aharon*, who, when he met the Saba Kadisha, made the blessing, "Blessed are You Who has apportioned of His knowledge to those who fear Him.")

Once, the *Pnei Yitzchak* was struck by a terrible illness. He could not speak or move any of his limbs, and the doctors despaired of his life. The Saba Kadisha came to visit him and told him, "I promise that Chacham Yitzchak will recover from this illness, but he has to believe in the power of my promise, and with this power he will recover and become healthy."

The *Pnei Yitzchak* answered, "Amen."

After a few days, the *Pnei Yitzchak* stood up and began walking around outside. Suddenly, the news spread that one of the *Pnei Yitzchak*'s relatives had taken ill that very day. Several days later, that man passed away.

Because he lived in the Saba Kadisha's neighborhood, the Saba Kadisha went to accompany his coffin several cubits, while the *Pnei Yitzchak* walked on his right. The *Pnei Yitzchak* told the Saba

Kadisha, "When his honor left after visiting me, this man began to laugh, saying about me, 'How is it possible for him to stand up from his bed and recover from this critical illness?' Now that I have recovered, thanks to the blessing of his honor the rav, this man has fallen to his bed and gone on to the next world."

The Saba Kadisha replied, "Be quiet, and do not tell anyone of this matter."

Later, the Saba Kadisha returned to Istanbul, and it is unknown exactly when he moved back to Damascus. From *Torah MiZion* it appears that in the year 5647/1887 he was still in Istanbul. In *Yatzeiv Gevulos* (about the Rabbi Meir Baal Haness funds, also known as *Mishpat VaTzedek*), a lengthy responsum is printed from the Saba Kadisha, and it appears that by the time of the printing (5664/1904), he was already rav in Damascus.

In Damascus, the Saba Kadisha ruled with a strong hand. He was appointed *Chacham Bashi,* or chief rabbi, and he was respected and loved by the king. He worked to strengthen Torah observance and to benefit the Jews, but he did not favor wealthy people in the slightest. On the contrary — he would rebuke them, just as he would rebuke anyone who did not listen to him.

Once, a certain Jew who was the main secretary of the governor became envious of him, and told some wealthy people, "I will arrange that the Saba Kadisha will have to come to me and beg for his life." He fabricated a document maligning the Saba Kadisha, intimidated prominent individuals who feared him into signing it, and gave it to the governor. When the Saba Kadisha was apprised of this matter, he had no choice but to go to the governor. When he entered the governor's palace, the sword-wielding guards were in awe of him, and allowed him to enter. He spoke to the governor courageously, and the governor himself escorted him to the door on his way out. Later, when the Jewish secretary came in, the governor ordered him to bring a letter from the Saba Kadisha stating that he was not upset at him. Otherwise, the governor told him, he would he would be expelled from the Turkish Empire.

The disgraced secretary took several prestigious people with him to the Saba Kadisha. But it was a Friday, and the Saba Kadisha told them that he did not have time to talk because Shabbos was coming. After Shabbos, the secretary came again to the Saba Kadisha's home to beg forgiveness. The Saba Kadisha answered that he would give him a note to save him and his family from expulsion, but that he would be punished for tormenting a Torah scholar so arrogantly.

Later, this man became blind.

TZEFAS

In Sivan of 5670/1910, the Saba Kadisha moved to the holy city of Tzefas, where he was the leader of the rabbanim and the leading spokesman, and the people were in awe of him.

Near his home was a group of G-d-fearing people who awoke in the middle of the night to delve into the secrets of the Torah. They testified that there was a pillar of fire on his house, and the sound of his Torah could be heard from a distance.

One Lag BaOmer, the people were afraid that the Arabs were going to prevent the celebration of the yahrtzeit of R' Shimon bar Yochai from taking place. The entire night of Lab BaOmer, a fire was seen burning in the Saba Kadisha's home, and the people were fearful about this. The next day, the Saba Kadisha sent for the Jews and told them, "I take it on my responsibility that you can make the celebration as usual." The celebration took place without any disturbance.

Someone came to speak to the Saba Kadisha one morning, but before he explained what he wanted, the Saba Kadisha said, "Look! This dreamer is coming! But do not be afraid." He then interpreted the dream favorably.

The person was astounded, for he had indeed come to inquire about a frightening dream, and the Saba Kadisha had interpreted it, with his Divine Inspiration, without even hearing what it was.

In Nissan of 5674/1914, after *Kiddush Levanah*, the Saba Kadisha clapped his hands together and tears streamed from his eyes. When he was asked about this, he answered that he sensed that there would be a great war in the world. That summer, World War I broke out.

During World War I, the Turks who ruled Eretz Yisrael were very powerful. The Saba Kadisha did not fear them, however, and he would speak harshly to them on behalf of the Jews.

Once, the great pasha, who was the general of the army, came to Tzefas, and all the high-ranking government officials went to greet him. The Saba Kadisha did not go with them, however. He went later, by himself. When the pasha asked him why he had not come with the government officials, he answered, "I will not go together with bandits." Afterwards, the pasha asked him for a blessing. The Saba Kadisha said, "A blessing requires humility, so the pasha must first dismount from his horse and then I will bless him."

The pasha did so and the Saba Kadisha blessed him, concluding, "If the pasha will look kindly upon the Jews and save them and guard them, Hashem will listen to his prayer."

It happened several times that Torah scholars came to the Saba Kadisha crying that they did not have any way to get out of army service. To each of them he said, "Do not go with them, and do not fear." In the end, these people were taken to Acco, but they were able to return from there miraculously.

Once, the Saba Kadisha had a very painful urinary tract infection. A doctor was summoned without his knowledge, and he said that surgery was necessary to save his life. The Saba Kadisha banished the doctor, saying that he believes in Hashem, the true Healer. The doctors laughed at him and despaired of his life if he did not obey them. In the end, he recovered fully, and the embarrassed doctors conceded that it was miraculous.

Expert doctors wanted to take him to Hadassah Hospital in Tzefas, but he refused to go, even after he was assured that the food was kosher and only male nurses would tend to him. He explained that he did not want people to say, "We made Avraham (i.e., himself) rich," when he did not wish to derive benefit from them or their money. He always said in similar situations, "No hand should touch me," for most of the medical staff were secular, and he could not abide such people.

R' Berish Zaltz did not have children for fifteen years after his wedding. One day, he had an argument with a certain person who belittled and cursed him, going as far as to say, "You are child-less, and childless you shall remain." These cruel words pierced R' Berish's heart, and tears poured from his eyes. He went to the Saba Kadisha right away to complain about this person, and the tzaddik listened to him pour out his embittered heart. After a few moments, the Saba Kadisha's face began to glow with happiness, and he told R' Berish excitedly, "Do not fear at all. With the help of Hashem, and with the power of our holy Torah, I promise you that this year you will have a son." And that year, his wife gave birth to a boy.

When we were in Tzefas, a certain Torah scholar descended from holy people told us that for many years he did not have children. He wanted to divorce his wife, but the *beis din* did not want him to do so, because she was known to be God-fearing and they had pity on her. The Sephardic *beis din* would not allow him to divorce her for the same reason. He was advised to go to the Saba Kadisha, the leader of the rabbanim, to arrange the divorce.

Rather than discuss the divorce, however, the Saba Kadisha told him, "Come to me on Purim." He did so, bringing porridge and wine. The Saba Kadisha then gave him his *shirayim* to drink and instructed that some be given to his wife as well. He told the man, "Have faith in Hashem that you will not need to separate, and that you will be blessed with surviving offspring." His wife had a son, and he showed us the child that had been born through the tzad-dik's blessing.

In Adar of 5681/1921, the Saba Kadisha left Tzefas and traveled to Teveriah and Jerusalem to consult with doctors. He also began printing some of his responsa in Jerusalem, but after several sizeable booklets had been finished, he stopped the printing in the middle for an unknown reason. He did not stop because of lack of funds, for he was not lacking for anything. (After the Saba Kadisha's passing, the Rebbe strongly desired to see these booklets, but they could not be found. Later, the booklets were found hidden at the burial cave of the *Levushei Serad* in Tzefas. They were sent to the Rebbe, and his spirit was revived.)

A wealthy Sephardic Jew pressured the Saba Kadisha to accept 200 Israeli liras to help cover the cost of printing his writings, but he refused the money on the grounds that the donor had no beard (even though he removed it with scissors, not with a razor). On another occasion, a generous woman who came to Tzefas sent him a sealed envelope containing 100 liras to print his works. He sent it back to her, however, writing that she should instead give it to charity or to Torah scholars.

He returned to Tzefas in 5683/1923. On 15 Elul 5685/1925 he traveled again to bathe in the healing springs of Teveriah, due to the illness from which he suffered for many years. He left all of his belongings and *sefarim* in Tzefas, for he intended to return. But Hashem ordained that his illness intensify, and he had to travel to Jerusalem to be treated in the hospital of Dr. Wallach. The sages of Jerusalem entreated him to settle there, and he acceded.

JERUSALEM

The following are some aspects of the Saba Kadisha's conduct and holy ways, as observed in Jerusalem in the last years of his life:

1. He would daven Shacharis at daybreak (*vasikin*) every day, even when he was weak. When he was hospitalized, although he suffered terribly all night, he mustered his strength to daven immediately after dawn.

2. He would wear two sets of tefillin at the same time, and he davened the entire Shacharis wearing them, as was the custom of the earlier Sephardic leaders.

3. Whenever he said a prayer or even a blessing over food, every word was permeated with fear of G-d and awe of His holiness.

4. He would stand throughout the *chazzan's* repetition of *Shemoneh Esrei* (see *Rema, Orach Chaim* 124:4).

5. He would daven the Friday evening service while it was still day. After Maariv he would go home and say *Shalom Aleichem*. He would then wait between one-and-a-half and two hours into the night, and then he would recite the *Shema* and make Kiddush.

6. Every Shabbos, he would be called to the Torah for the sixth *aliyah*. At the end of his life, when there was a *minyan* in his home, he himself honored the people with the *aliyos*.

7. He was very insistent that no more than seven people be called to the Torah on Shabbos (see *Magen Avraham, Orach Chaim* 282 §1).

8. On *Shabbos Bereishis*, five people were called up to the Torah during the first section of the Torah reading. The Kohen was called up for the reading about the first day of Creation, the Levi was called up for the reading of the second day, and so on. For the reading of the sixth day, he was called up, and before the blessing he said, "*B'simna tava* (in a good omen)." Then he would read the Torah again from the beginning of *Parashas Bereishis* until the words "*bara Elokim laasos.*"

9. On Rosh Hashanah and Yom Kippur, he davened for the *amud* all of the prayers of the day.

10. On the evening of Yom Kippur, before *Kol Nidrei*, he followed Ramban's custom of reciting the great *Vidui* when he came to shul (see *Nimukei Orach Chaim* 607).

11. He himself recited *Kol Nidrei* the first time, in the traditional Sephardic tune. For the second and third recitations, he honored the two scholars standing at his right and left.

12. He made *hakafos* on the night of Shemini Atzeres (which is Simchas Torah in Eretz Yisrael), and during the day as well, after Mussaf and during Minchah. On the night of Motza'ei Yom Tov (which is Simchas Torah outside of Eretz Yisrael)[2] and on *Shabbos Bereishis* after Mussaf, he danced by himself, holding a small *Sefer Torah* written on deerskin parchment. (He said that it was an ancient custom of the sages of Istanbul to make *hakafos* on *Shabbos Bereishis*.) He was very particular that someone should stand holding a *Sefer Torah* near

---

2. See *Shaar Yissas'char* II, *Maamarei Chodesh Tishrei, Maamar Zeman Simchaseinu* 28.

the *bimah* during the *hakafos*, so that the people would encircle the *bimah* and the *Sefer Torah*.[3]

13. All his Torah study was to clarify the practical halachah. When he was told that a certain sage knew the entire Torah by heart, he said, "The main thing is not study, but action."

14. He was proficient in all areas of the Torah, and he knew *Shas, Poskim, Rishonim,* and *Acharonim* by heart. He would give answers without looking into *sefarim*, because his memory was so phenomenal that he never forgot anything. Only when he was writing *divrei Torah* for print did he instruct that they be checked to be sure he quoted the sources correctly.

15. His principal Torah study was at night — although his immersion in Torah study during the day was also astounding.

16. His eyesight was so clear that he did not need spectacles, and his eyes did not weaken until his last moments. He would write prolific Torah works and novellae with his own holy hand.

17. At the end of his life he barely ate. During the week, he would not eat an olive-sized portion of bread, nor would he wash his hands to eat. He washed only to eat Shabbos and Yom Tov meals.

18. He was stringent not to eat anything that required checking [for insects] or any food whose permissibility was even the slightest bit questionable. He was not lenient in this matter even when he was ill and suffering greatly at the end of his life.

19. He was also very stringent about the *bein hashmashos* (twilight) period, even with regard to rabbinic prohibition, such as eating after Tishah B'Av. Even when he was ill, he did not eat or taste anything after the fast until 72 minutes after sunset.

20. He strove to conceal his actions and be exceedingly modest. He knew his own greatness, but he was nev-

---

3. See *Chida, Avodas HaKodesh: Tziporen Shamir.*

ertheless very humble and fled from honor. When he traveled, he did not wish to divulge the time of his trip so that people would not escort him and disrupt his schedule.

21. There were many days and weeks when he would seclude himself in his house and not see anyone. No one knows what he did then.

22. Generally, he did not shake anyone's hand, even that of *gedolei Yisrael*. On rare occasions, he would shake the hands of very special individuals. He explained simply that handshaking was a new custom that came from the secular countries, and in earlier times, the custom was only to say *"Shalom"* verbally. He also had deeper reasons for this (see *Divrei Torah* 6:13).

23. He did not derive benefit from anyone, nor did he accept any charity or financial support from private individuals or the public. He hated gifts. Even when people wished to fill his pockets with gold, he did not value money and he did not accept it. He, however, would give to others, from the time he was young until his old age.

24. He was very particular about not following European time, since that system of calculating time starts at midnight, when the founder of Christianity was born. He would tell time only by Eretz Yisrael time, which begins in the evening. He would say that this follows the holy Torah's rule (*Bereishis* 1:5), "And there was evening, and there was morning, one day" — i.e., the day begins in the evening.

25. In his lectures, he would rebuke freely, not favoring anyone. Nevertheless, no one held this against him, for they knew that he was motivated by truth.

26. His entire life he persecuted and abhorred those scholars and rabbanim who abetted and curried favor with evildoers. He would say, "The sinners are sinners, but the flatterers are the ones who create sinners. They are worse than the sinners themselves." If such flatterers

would come to him, he would speak disparagingly to them, and he would refuse to answer their questions in Torah matters. "I do not worship the *Markulis* (i.e., a form of idol worship)," he would say. He would distance himself as much as possible from those who were known to be sinners and from those who caused the public to sin. "Go out, impure ones," he would tell them, "and do not come to see my face."

When the Rebbe was in Jerusalem, great rabbanim came to consult with him about a certain flagrant transgression that had been perpetrated in the Holy City. The Rebbe asked the Saba Kadisha what to do about this, and he answered that there was reason to be cautious, and it was therefore better to do nothing at the moment. He then offered a beautiful homiletic explanation of the Talmud's statement (*Yoma* 76b): *Chamra v'reichani pikchin*, wine and fragrance sharpen the intellect. In the context of the ketores (the incense offered in the Beis HaMikdash), we find that the sound of a voice is beneficial to fragrant spices. We also find (*Menachos* 87a) that speech is harmful to wine. The Sages alluded to this idea, explained the Saba Kadisha, with their teaching that *chamra* (wine), representing the times when it is appropriate not to speak, and *reichani* (fragrance), representing the times when it is appropriate to speak, should be left to the *pikchin*, the wise people of the generation, to deliberate and decide. Sometimes, it is necessary to speak up; other times, it is best to be silent.

The Saba Kadisha also told the Rebbe, "When the students of a certain yeshivah came to my house to discuss Torah matters and I saw that they did not have a beard or side locks and they grew their frontal hair, I expounded before them the verse (*Shir HaShirim* 2:14), 'Show Me your countenance, let me hear your voice' — first show me that your appearance is in the image of G-d, the way the Torah teaches, and only then I will listen to your Torah. Otherwise, I will not speak to you.

"I rebuffed them because they are the destroyers of the Holy City. That is what the Rebbe should do, as well. He should caution his chassidim and G-d-fearing people to stay away from these people, but they should not protest loudly now about this matter."

Once, when the city leaders came to him, he rebuked them for standing idly by at a time when the Torah was being violated. "There is nothing we can do," they answered. "In this wanton generation, only Hashem can bring salvation and raise the banner of Torah."

The Saba Kadisha was not pleased with their answer, and referred to the discussion in the Talmud (*Sotah* 49b) about what will happen at the end of days. "The face of the generation will be like the face of a dog, the wisdom of the learned ones will rot, brazenness will be rampant," etc. The statement, "On whom can we rely? On our Father in Heaven" appears several times in that discussion.

"Why," the Saba Kadisha asked, "does the Talmud insert this almost poetic statement right in the middle of listing all of the sorrows that will be at the end of days? Is it not a great blessing that the people will have faith in Hashem?

"Had the Talmud been offering advice to the people living at the end of days, it would have said, 'On whom should they rely,' not, 'On whom can we rely.' The Talmud's intention was that this statement is also one of the curses and sorrows of the generation. When you ask the leaders of the generation why they are silent when they should be rebuking their contemporaries for their brazenness and for the other negative attributes listed by the Talmud, they will answer, 'We have no one to rely on but our Father in Heaven; we cannot do anything.' This will be their excuse for not protesting, and the misdeeds of the generation will then be blamed on them. If the leaders conduct themselves this way, there is no greater curse. A person has free choice, and a leader must protest with all his might. Even a weak person must become a mighty warrior to protect that which is holy and not, God forbid, excuse himself by saying that the situation cannot be rectified."

When I sent R' Asher Zelig Margulies, author of Ashrei HaIsh, a copy of the Rebbe's inspiring *divrei Torah* that he said at the time of the recitation of the *Hoshanos* on Hoshana Rabbah 5689/1929, he read them to the Saba Kadisha, who enjoyed them very much. He said that this is how it should be — the tzaddik of the generation should rebuke the people for their sins and cry out bitterly that they should repent.

He then quoted the explanation offered by R' Yaakov Kuli (who arranged and edited the *Mishneh L'Melech*) on the verse (*Bereishis* 18:26), "If I find in Sodom fifty tzaddikim in the midst of the city, then I would spare the entire place on their account." The words "in the midst of the city" seem superfluous. The verse means to say, "It is not difficult to find tzaddikim who sit in their homes, alone, and devote themselves to Torah and mitzvos," the Saba Kadisha explained. "It is far more difficult to find righteous people who are 'in the midst of the city' — in the marketplaces and the streets, enacting safeguards, repairing breaches, and influencing people to repent. Those are the type of tzaddikim that Avraham was referring to, for those tzaddikim have the ability to stop the evil and thereby protect their city from destruction."

In *Iyov* (1:7), we find that when Hashem asked Satan where he was coming from, he answered, "From wandering and walking about the earth." The Saba Kadisha explained that in earlier years, it was difficult for Satan to convince people to sin, for who was foolish enough to listen to him and violate Hashem's word and His Torah? Satan had to work hard and employ all sorts of tactics to convince people that a misdeed was actually a mitzvah, or at least a "sin for the sake of Heaven." Nowadays, however, it is much easier for people to be convinced to sin. That is what the Satan meant when he answered, "I am coming from wandering and walking about the earth" — I no longer need to stay in one place for a long time until people listen to me; all I need to do is simply wander around and pass by, and people immediately come running after me to sin. They answer me almost before I call them, saying, "We will do and we will listen" (heard from the chassid R' Avraham Fried of Nanash, when he was in Jerusalem in 5689/1929 and brought a letter from the Rebbe to the Saba Kadisha).

When the Rebbe arrived in Jerusalem and went to daven at the Kosel HaMaaravi, R' Meir Arzi (owner of the house where the Saba Kadisha lived) hurried to notify the Saba Kadisha that he had fulfilled his mission faithfully by delivering his letter to the Rebbe.

He also told him with satisfaction of the honor that had been accorded to the Rebbe in Lod.

When he finished, the Saba Kadisha sighed sadly. R' Meir was very frightened by this sigh, for everything he had told the Saba Kadisha was good. He mustered the courage to ask why the Saba Kadisha had sighed. He answered, "If only his departure could be like his arrival." R' Meir still did not understand, but he did not ask any more questions. He did not tell anyone about this exchange until the day the Saba Kadisha passed away, which was the day before the Rebbe's departure from the Holy Land. Only then did he understand these words that had been said with Divine Inspiration.

The Saba Kadisha's greatness and powerful acts are inscribed upon the hearts of those who came to him to seek God during his lifetime. But most of his achievements and greatness are unknown, for he concealed himself, except at the end of his life when he became somewhat renowned. If our generation is worthy of having his many manuscripts printed, that will allow us a glimpse at his great wisdom in all areas of Torah. But who knows if the world will merit seeing his writings printed in the near future, since he did not leave behind any descendants to see to this matter. Moreover, immediately after he passed away, before we left Eretz Yisrael, we heard that his writings and his library were in alien hands, in the possession of some official rabbis who did not protect the honor of the Torah and did not appreciate the value of these holy works. It is indeed a loss that these works were not published right away. Nevertheless, the lips of this holy tzaddik whisper in the grave. May he be a defending angel to bring much good to us and to all the Jewish people, until the arrival of the Redeemer, may it be speedily in our days.